MW00437620

Sex So Great
She Can't Get Enough

Sex So Great
She Can't Get Enough

Barbara Keesling, Ph.D.

M. EVANS

Lanham • New York • Boulder • Toronto • Plymouth, UK

Published by M. Evans
An imprint of The Rowman & Littlefield Publishing Group, Inc.
4501 Forbes Boulevard, Suite 200, Lanham, Maryland 20706
www.rowman.com

10 Thornbury Road, Plymouth PL6 7PP, United Kingdom

Distributed by National Book Network

British Library Cataloguing in Publication Information Available

**The hardback edition of this book was previously cataloged by the
Library of Congress as follows:**

Keesling, Barbara.
    Sex so great she can't get enough / Barbara Keesling.
        p. cm.
    1. Sex instruction for men. I. Title.
    HQ36.K445 2005
    613.9′6′081—dc22   2005008483

    ISBN 978-1-59077-092-4 (cloth : alk. paper)
    ISBN 978-1-59077-206-5 (pbk. : alk. paper)

∞™ The paper used in this publication meets the minimum
requirements of American National Standard for Information Sciences—
Permanence of Paper for Printed Library Materials, ANSI/NISO
Z39.48-1992.

Printed in the United States of America

contents

introduction

Every man I've ever met wants to feel confident that he is a fantastic lover. He wants to look at his partner and know from the expression in her eyes, the softness of her mouth, and the glow on her skin that she has been satisfied, as well as turned on. Totally! What man doesn't want that? And why shouldn't he? What is more amazing than being with a lover who feels as though she is coming alive by something you are doing to her body? What's more exciting than being with a sexual partner and knowing exactly what to do with your own body, hands, mouth, and penis?

What makes a man a great lover has little or nothing to do with the size of his penis or the shape of his butt. It has everything to do with his passion, his enthusiasm, and his willingness to love and learn a woman's body. It has everything to do with his being self-confident enough to learn so much about the opposite sex that he knows exactly how their bodies work. It has everything to do with his capacity to be sexually open. It has everything to do with his understanding of sex and all its components. Sex can be steamy; sex can be hot; sex can be playful; sex can be comforting; sex can be loving; and sex can be friendly. Sex is one of the simplest things any of us ever do; it is also one of the most complex. It's up to us to take advantage of our natural sexual feelings and explore all the ways in which sex can bring us pleasure and make us feel good about life in general.

I BELIEVE IN FANTASTIC SEX!

If you're reading this book, you probably agree with me. Life is too short, and sex is too important for us to waste time being confused about how to make our sex lives better. It's my job as a therapist to help you, as a healthy sexual being, to take charge of your sex life and make it everything you always wanted it to be—and more. Before going any further though, let me tell you a little bit about my history. Let me tell you why I know enough to give you the sexual information you need.

I admit it: I've always been interested in sex. But when I graduated from high school, I certainly didn't think, "When I grow up, I want to be a sex therapist." I was a naïve young woman from a small town in Southern California, and I wasn't exactly sure what I wanted to be. So I got a job at the U.S. Post Office. I wore a post office uniform; I had a postal bag; and I drove a postal Jeep. I even had a small vial of pepper spray hooked onto my belt in case I ever met a particularly unfriendly dog. Driving around and delivering the usual run of magazines, utility bills, and inviting postcards from far-off places gave me a lot of time to think about what I wanted to do with my life. Occasionally, I would look down at a particularly inviting postcard depicting a beach in Hawaii or a vineyard in the South of France and think, "Well, I could move there, but how would I make a living?" As you can imagine, my job was not giving me much inspiration.

One day during my lunch break, I was sitting in a diner eating a chili cheese omelet and home fries (carrying mail is a tough job; you can't do it on tofu) and reading the lifestyle section of a local newspaper. I spotted an article about sexual surrogate partners. By the time I was halfway through the article, I knew that this was something that interested me. "This is the career for me," I said to myself. So I applied for a job at a clinic run by established sex therapists. Within a short time, I had discarded my mail carrier uniform for good.

I don't know how much you know about what it means to be a sexual surrogate. It means that first you receive training and then work with therapists to help men and women with their sexual issues and concerns. Typically, a sex therapist assigns a surrogate to someone who is having sexual difficulties and who doesn't have a sexual partner. As you can imagine, unattached singles are at a particular disadvantage in resolving sexual issues. Sometimes they have issues they want to work through before they feel confident enough to try to find a partner. Surrogate partners coach their clients, frequently doing this by guiding clients as an intimate, hands-on coach and teacher. This is serious, sincere work. The first qualification for doing this work is that you be accepting and non-judgmental. People who are having serious sexual problems typically don't fully understand what is going wrong; a surrogate partner can provide the professional support and understanding they need.

As a surrogate, I listened, talked, instructed, and often participated. When I first took the job, you can imagine that my friends and family were a little bit surprised. Many were frankly shocked. Others couldn't resist teasing and making jokes whenever they saw me. One person thought so little of my sexual appeal that he said, "You're going to starve." But I didn't mind what people said because I found the work incredibly interesting and gratifying. I really felt as though I was making a difference in people's lives; my job was ultimately helping them form and keep loving, happy relationships.

When people are unable to have satisfying sex lives, they can be incredibly unhappy. My work as a surrogate partner gave me great insight into how important sex is; it also showed me how our whole outlook and attitude can be changed by learning how to use and enjoy our bodies.

Being a sexual surrogate also inspired me to return to school so I could do more work in the field. I completed my undergraduate work; I finished my master's degree; and I got a doctorate. I have been working as a sex therapist and counselor ever since, teaching in colleges and universities in California and working in private practice.

I KNOW A LOT ABOUT SEX

After more than twenty years studying, working, and teaching in the sex field, I think I can say with confidence that I know more about sex than just about anybody. As a surrogate, I observed the sexual practices of hundreds of men firsthand. I know a lot about male sexuality, and I also know a lot about female sexuality. I've talked to more people about their sexual experiences than I can even begin to count. They have spoken with me honestly and openly. I've worked with many of these men and women, helping them resolve their sexual issues. I've seen how they were confused or sexually miseducated. I've shown people exactly how to satisfy themselves and each other. I've seen men and women who didn't know an orgasm from a cabbage patch go from cold potatoes to hot tomatoes. It's fun being able to do this because it makes such a difference.

Currently, I teach human sexuality to college students and have done so for many years. I've taught thousands of students; every year, hundreds of them ask me questions and share their intimate sexual concerns with me. As far as sex is concerned, I know what men and women know, don't know, want to know, and absolutely can't live without knowing.

I love helping people become more informed about sexual pleasure. No matter how good your sex life already is, I know it can become better. No matter how satisfied your partner is, I know she can discover new ways to find pleasure for herself and you. I want you to become the kind of man about whom women say, "Wow, he is some amazing lover!" That's what this book is all about.

A few years back, I wrote a book about male multiple orgasm called *How to Make Love All Night*. I had no idea how successful that book would be, and in the intervening years, I've received a great deal of correspondence from men asking me to write more books directed specifically to men's sexual issues. This book addresses these issues as well as providing men with a crash course in male multiple orgasm.

Did you ever look at your partner when you were making love and wonder why you seemed to be having more fun than she was? Or did you ever look at your partner while you were making love and wonder why she seemed to be getting more out of it than you were? Whether you are going to bed with someone for the first time or the five hundred and first time, *Sex So Great She Can't Get Enough* will help you add intimacy, zest, and passion to all your sexual encounters. It doesn't matter if your sex life is good, so-so, or even has its moments of greatness. It can be better!

Sexuality involves the whole person, not just the genitals; this book will address how we think and feel about sex, as well as the physical mechanics of making our bodies do what we want.

chapter one

MAKE YOUR PENIS YOUR PAL

Think you're the genius of your penis? Think again! In this chapter, I'm going to give you some advanced information about the care and pampering of your penis—how to treat it right so that it gives both you and your intimate partner unlimited pleasure. If you want to become the kind of lover a woman fantasizes about, you first need to understand more about yourself as a sexual being: your mind, your emotions, your body, your sexual history, and your penis.

Give yourself permission to start thinking about sex in a new way. Think about how you want to be in bed; think about what you want to do to please your partner. Take your time and give it some serious thought. When you're having sex with a woman, you want to be able to relax and fully enjoy the experience. That process starts by relaxing and taking your time as you think about sex. Being the best lover starts with you being able to explore and experience your sexual passion and pleasure. It starts with you!

If you're like most men, you discovered masturbation by the time you reached adolescence. It was intensely pleasurable so you probably did it again, and again, and again. In all likelihood, you have brought yourself to orgasm so many times that you consider yourself the expert on how your penis works. Well, sometimes you are; but not always. The problem is that most men approach sex without realistically thinking about the mechanics of the penis or what it is capable of doing. I want to change that attitude. I want you to be fully informed, and I want to help you use that information to give you total confidence and skill.

Let's start by taking a short trip down memory lane. While you're doing this, I'd like you to reflect on your own life and how your approach to sex evolved. As the adolescent male begins to mature sexually, what tends to happen is that he finds a method (or fantasy) that suits his style and, pardon the expression, he sticks with it. Some men, for example, began masturbating with a magazine or even a video that they "lifted" from their dad's sock drawer when they were still kids. Often a particular image or sexual fantasy became stuck in their heads. They got into the habit of touching themselves in the same way every time. Hey, it worked, so why not? Eventually, they graduated and began having sex with real multidimensional girls instead of (again pardon the expression) four-color spreads. With a real girl, things could get real confusing. They had to worry about whether she would say yes, and if she did say yes, whether or not they could satisfy her. And—this is very important—they also weren't really sure about how to make the transition from masturbation to intimate sexual experiences.

I've talked to hundreds of men about their first experiences with masturbation as well as their first sexual experience with real-life partners. Here are some typical examples:

"I was sixteen, but already I felt like I had been horny for my whole life. I took this girl to a drive-in movie. It was our first date, and I had no hope or expectation of having sex. When she suggested we get in the back seat, I couldn't believe it. I was so surprised when she guided my penis inside her that I didn't know what to do. I just lay there like a lox. I must have lasted all of a minute and a third."

"I must have been all of fifteen and this older girl (seventeen) from down the block and I had been having heavy make-out sessions all summer. Finally, one day I was in her house when her parents weren't home. She pulled me down on top of her on the couch. The instant my penis entered her, I was so completely unprepared for what I felt—the warmth, the wetness—that I came immediately. The orgasm was one of the best of my life. It was so intense that I still remember it vividly."

It goes without saying that the average young guy who is beginning to explore his sexuality doesn't feel that he has that much control over his penis, but what he lacks in experience he makes up for in enthusiasm. With that in mind, chances are that he just plunges forward and does the best he can. But, in the process, the typical guy can establish many habits relating to how he has sex and these habits can stay with him for a lifetime. As some men mature, they meet lovers who are more experimental and are able to affect some of their patterns and "moves." However, there are many others who just go forward and establish long-term relationships, clinging to the same methods they used when they were twenty-one. Years later, they are still doing it the same way and while it's good, it's not quite as fabulous as they would like it to be. In the process of all this, some men develop hang-ups and problems; others have issues with desire; still others become just plain bored and, in the process, become boring lovers.

I want this book to help male readers develop the same enthusiasm you had for your penis when you were fourteen years old, but I want that enthusiasm to be combined with skill, knowledge, expertise, and confidence. I want you to really be a genius of your penis. I can show you how to do this.

IT'S NOT A BONE. IT'S NOT A MUSCLE. IT'S ERECTILE TISSUE!

Do you know why your penis gets erect? Here's some information you need: Your penis has three cylinders of tissue; when you get excited, the arteries leading to your penis widen, blood flows into these cylinders, and voilà, an erection occurs! Your penis responds to two different types of sexual stimulation: When your penis receives physical stimulation—touching, stroking, kissing, sucking—it reacts by having an erection. It also responds to mental stimulation. Think about the times you had a spontaneous erection when you were looking—only looking—at a sensual woman (the real thing or a photograph) or having a fantasy of someone you wanted to have sex with. The best erections happen when you are being stimulated both mentally and physically.

Many men expect that they will get a spontaneous erection the instant they are with a naked woman. This just isn't true of everybody. Every man is different. There are men who continue to have spontaneous erections (erections with no direct physical stimulation) their entire lives, and there are other men (even young men) who always require some direct stimulation and never have spontaneous erections. Both responses are normal! There is nothing wrong, no matter how old or young you are, if you need some physical stimulation to help you get an erection.

Your erection response is very sensitive to stress. The erection response is not really under your voluntary control. You don't have to "try" to get an erection. In fact, trying will put more pressure on you and probably make it less likely that you will have an erection. Let me explain a little about the anatomy of the penis.

While you may refer to your penis as your "love muscle," the penis itself doesn't contain any muscles. However, there is a muscle group that surrounds the base of the penis. It's called the pubococcygeal muscle group (PC for short, but don't confuse it with your personal computer). You may have heard about the PC muscle in conjunction with female sexuality. Women are encouraged to do PC muscle exercises called "Kegels" to make their vaginas tighter and prepare for childbirth.

For many years, it was believed that the PC muscle was very important for women, but not so much so for men. I remember once reading an article by one of the most famous sex researchers in the country who said the PC muscle was of no importance for male sexual response. This couldn't be further from the truth; fortunately, we've learned more about what the PC muscle is capable of doing.

The PC muscle is the muscle group that spasms when you have an orgasm and ejaculation. In order to get an erection, the PC muscle at the base of your penis has to be relaxed. In fact, this is one of the ways that Viagra works: it helps relax that muscle group so that blood can flow into the penis. If you tense up your PC muscle to try to get an erection, you will actually prevent it from happening. In the next chapter, there are some exercises that will show you how to locate this muscle and make it stronger.

Erections and arousal aren't the same thing. Erection is how hard your penis is, and arousal is how close you are to orgasm and ejaculation. You could really be aroused, and even so, your erection might not be very hard. Or you could be rock hard, but feel like you're a million miles away from having an orgasm. A friend of mine likens the sensation of feeling that your ejaculation is retreating farther and farther into the future to "chasing the ice cream truck." Another man I know says that when that happens to him, the woman he's with invariably thinks he is a man who can "last" forever, but he knows that he's just a guy who's not going to have an orgasm.

I like to think of erections as having four stages:

1. **Initiation.** This is the preliminary phase when you first receive a sexual stimulus and you tell yourself that it's okay to go ahead with an erection.

2. **Filling.** This is when the blood starts to make its way into the penis and the penis thickens. On a scale of 1–10, 1 would signify no erection, and 2–4 would signify the process of blood filling the penis.

3. **Rigidity.** At the base of the penis are small valves located in the blood circulation system. Rigidity is reached when there is sufficient blood in the penis for the valves to get the message to begin to close off and trap the blood in the penis. On that 1–10 scale, the beginning of rigidity would measure 5 while levels 6–10 describe a penis that is reaching the upper limits of rigidity. At this stage, if you push down on your erect penis, it will spring back.

4. **Maintenance.** This describes a phase during which the valves at the base of the penis close off and the penis is able to maintain an erection. Sometimes a penis will stay erect even without direct stimulation, but many men require physical contact in order to maintain their erections.

One of the things all men should know is that erections often get harder and softer during the course of having sex. Sometimes the slightest feeling of softness is enough to make a man worry that something is going wrong. What typically happens is that the man then starts working harder to keep his erection. Usually, this has totally the opposite effect. If you feel that your erection is getting weaker, the best thing you can do is relax, breathe, and enjoy what your partner is doing. Enjoy her touch, enjoy her skin, and enjoy her enjoyment. Forget about your penis and your erection for a moment and focus on the sensuality of the moment. If you relax and get back into the total sensuality of what you are doing, the chances are extremely good that your erection will respond accordingly.

ENJOY YOUR PENIS

If you are going to get optimum pleasure from sex, you need to start by becoming more comfortable with everything about it. You have to stop worrying about how thick your penis is, how long it is, and how it looks. Accept your penis for what it is, and you and the women in your life will be significantly more satisfied.

PENIS RULE #1: Attitude is everything.

Your attitude toward your penis will determine *her* attitude toward your penis. Look at that sentence and repeat it to yourself. Memorize it. Then say it again. Your partner can't help but be affected by your attitude toward your penis, and it will be reflected in her own satisfaction and lovemaking. Any woman will tell you that the best lovers are confident lovers. Most of that confidence comes from being relaxed about your penis and what it is doing.

Ask yourself how you think about your penis. Do you monitor what it is doing and treat it as though it literally has a life of its own? During sex, for example, do you think things like: "Oh look at my penis (or whatever word you use), it's really performing well tonight"? Or, "Why isn't it getting hard?"

Do you have a secret or "pet" name for your penis? Is it a personal name connected to your own like ("little" or "big" Howie), a name that conveys power ("The Rock" or "The Terminator"), a name that conveys pleasure ("Mr. Happy"), a humorous name ("Elmo"), or a name that conveys ambivalence or negativity ("Mr. Droopy")? Stop to think what effect your penis's pet name may have on your attitude toward sex. Think about what effect your pet name will have on a woman. "The Terminator" may scare her. "Mr. Droopy" will probably scare her as well. If you want to call your penis something, make it something that denotes pleasure. And it goes without saying, never ever apologize for your penis.

Always remember that your penis is a part of who you are. Men who emphasize performance frequently think about the penis as though it is an independent object. As a sex therapist, one of the most important things I do with men is to try to help them erase a performance-based attitude toward sex. A mantra that I repeat often is, "Sex is about pleasure, not performance."

We all know that the sexual act is a complete and integrated experience, but we don't always act that way. For most men, the primary reason they fail to grasp the full-body nature of sex is that they don't know how to relax. They start out stressed and worried about performance, and they stay that way. Tension and old lovemaking habits keep them from enjoying the moment-by-moment sensations.

The most experienced and sexual women in the world will tell you that if you are confident and comfortable about your penis, you can be a fabulous lover even when your penis isn't doing exactly what you want it to do. Women are made uncomfortable by a man who acts unsure of himself and worries about his erection. But women are made secure and turned on by a man who forgets about his erection (or lack thereof) and uses his hands, fingers, mouth, skin, and whatever he has to give and get pleasure.

So the first thing to do if you want your penis to give you and your partner pleasure is relax. Being relaxed makes you appear confident and sexier, which in turn gives you real sexual power.

PENIS RULE #2: If a woman likes you, she likes your penis.

A woman wants to feel your penis inside of her because it's part of you, not because it's a particular size or shape. Men are sometimes under the impression that "women like dick" in general, without making any distinctions about the men to whom these "dicks" are attached. That's rarely true. The typical woman's sexual desire is directed at a particular object (person) and when she pictures having great sex, she pictures it with this person. Responding to what your penis does is part of her general responsiveness to you. This is true no matter what your shape or size. When a woman tells you, "I just want to feel *you!*" she means it. That's because women have a different hormonal balance than men.

Testosterone, sometimes referred to as a male hormone, is largely responsible for sex drive. Testosterone is the reason why a man's voice is deeper than a woman, and it's also the reason why men are more sexually driven in general. For the most part, the more testosterone a man produces, the more interested he is in sex. Men produce testosterone throughout their lives, but it diminishes as they get older; libido tends to diminish accordingly. A typical man of seventy will be less sexually motivated than a typical man of twenty.

Some women do have more testosterone than others. As an interesting side note, women for whom doctors have prescribed testosterone typically report increased libido and sexuality. The late Theresa Crenshaw, M.D., a noted sex researcher and therapist, theorized that women have a variety of different types of sexual desire to correspond to different hormones. According to her research, testosterone was responsible for a woman's aggressive sex drive, but she thought that a woman's urge to "seduce" and attract a man was regulated by estrogen, dopamine, and oxytocin (the so-called bonding hormone). Her research also indicated that a woman's desire to be penetrated or be the passive partner during intercourse was influenced by high levels of estrogen and serotonin. Many women describe these different kinds of feeling surrounding sex drive and sexual desire.

men, not women, worry about size and shape

It's the very rare case where a man's penis and a woman's vagina don't mesh well from the standpoint of size. Nonetheless, many men obsess about penis size; the typical belief is that it looks too small when it's not erect. These same men often think their penis looks okay when it is erect. If you have this obsession to the point where it's interfering with your sexual enjoyment, you really need to get over it! Most men have penises that look smaller when they are not erect.

There is a lot of myth and advertising propaganda surrounding penis size. Just this morning, I received at least half a dozen pieces of e-mail spam of the BE BIGGER AND HARDER OVERNIGHT variety. My advice is to not take any of this too seriously. Although some doctors advertise "male enhancement" surgeries, current techniques for penile enlargement surgeries generally don't work very well for reasons that have to do with the blood supply to the penis. I once asked the rhetorical question in my class: "So given that penile enlargement surgery generally doesn't work, what should a man do if he genuinely believes that his penis is too small?" One student piped up, "Buy a big truck," which I thought was as good an answer as any.

There are two ways to enlarge a penis surgically. In the first procedure, the surgeon loosens or cuts the ligaments that anchor the penis to the pubic bone. This makes the penis look as though it is longer when it is flaccid. There can be a problem with cutting these ligaments because then, when a man gets an erection, it might tend to "swivel."

A way to make a penis thicker or wider is to inject a substance into the space between the skin and the *tunica albuginia*, the membrane that holds the three cylinders of erectile tissue together. Substances that have been injected in the past include collagen and silicone. Currently doctors use autologous fat (fat from your own body). They usually get the fat by doing liposuction on your love handles. The problem with this procedure is that gravity often makes the injected fat clump up on the underside of the penis. Often, two or three treatments are necessary in order to even the fat out. Even so, it can come out looking like a lumpy potato.

Sometimes men say things to me like, "Well, a friend of mine swears that he uses something that makes his penis bigger when he's having sex. Do you know of anything like that?"

Well, I don't know anyone with a computer who doesn't receive one or dozens of e-mails daily from companies promising that one method or another can make men "bigger."

One gizmo that some men have used is a vacuum erection device (Swedish Penis Enlarger). This is a clear plastic cylinder that fits over the penis and is attached to a small pump. When you press the pump, a vacuum is created in the cylinder, drawing blood into the penis. The cylinder comes with a small medical rubber band that you slip over the penis and leave in place while you are having sex. The band acts like a cock ring and holds blood in the penis. The vacuum erection pump is a medical device that's used in sex therapy with older men who may have difficulty maintaining an erection; it's also sold as a novelty in adult stores and used by younger men who swear it increases penis length. What happens is that if you use it for twenty minutes every day, it can give you the appearance of more length because it trains you to have a little more blood in your penis than you usually do. If you want to use this kind of device with a partner, it would probably be a good idea to tell the woman because she will probably be able to feel the rubber band. Some women can find it causes chafing or irritation. There was recently a story in the news about a judge here in this country who was using the vacuum erection device under his robes during court proceedings. People heard the swooshing sound. I swear I'm not making this up.

There are some other things you should know before you use a vacuum pump to improve your erection: Don't keep it on for more than twenty minutes because it functions as a sort of tourniquet and can damage your erectile tissue. Also, be cautious about where you place the rubber band. Placing it directly over a vein can cause bleeding. Plus, this device is not recommended if you have difficulty ejaculating.

There are conditions that can cause unusually small penises. An adult penis that's less than an inch long when erect is a medical condition called microphallus. It usually occurs in conjunction with other serious birth defects. There's also something called a hidden or concealed penis. This can occur when a man becomes so overweight that he develops a fat pad in the lower abdomen that literally engulfs the shaft of the penis. The penis is still there, but you can't see it. It looks weird, but it doesn't affect your sex life that much. A man with this condition has to reach inside and pull out the penis to urinate or have intercourse. The only time it protrudes by itself is when there is an erection. (This problem can be resolved with surgery.)

Beyond size, there's another concern about penis appearance that comes up for men and that's circumcision. There are two issues here. One is aesthetics. In general, women do not have a preference for circumcised versus uncircumcised penises. Individual women may prefer one over the other, but while having sexual intercourse, most women report that both feel the same.

A second issue is sensitivity. Some men believe that because they were circumcised as infants, they were genitally mutilated without their consent. The attitude toward mandatory circumcision is starting to change because it's not necessary or even beneficial from a medical standpoint. But some men believe that their penises would be either more or less sensitive if they weren't circumcised. There is no research to support the idea that circumcision impacts on a man's sexual performance.

CARING FOR YOUR PENIS

When I tell you to be relaxed about your penis, I don't want to give the impression that I think you should ignore it. Quite the contrary.

PENIS RULE #3: Pay attention to your penis!

You can't just ignore your penis and only pay attention to it when you're masturbating or having sex! I can't talk about the penis without reminding you that it needs care. Jerry Seinfeld does a bit about how everybody spends more time washing their genitals than any other part of their body so I probably don't need to tell you about regular showering. You shouldn't scrub it so hard that your skin becomes irritated, but you want it to be clean and attractive. If you're not circumcised, that means that you need to pull the foreskin back every day and wash under it to make sure that you don't get an infection. Cleanliness is also essential for your partner's health and well being.

A question I'm sometimes asked concerns how soon after sex should you get up to wash off your penis. Well, some women do complain about men who wash off too soon, and others complain about men who don't wash soon (or often) enough. Many women find it a real turn-off, for example, when a man hops out of bed within seconds of sex to wash himself off. This is an off-putting mood-breaker for women who like to cuddle after sex (and most women like to cuddle after sex). On the other hand, women also complain about men who have had one orgasm and then initiate oral sex without washing themselves off. This is particularly true if the couple has been using a birth control method that includes spermicide. It has a nasty taste!

Something that helps keep the penis looking appealing and attractive is to rub Vaseline around the head on a daily basis. It keeps the skin soft and lubricated. You can also massage the area beneath the head of your penis with Vaseline. Just use a little bit.

Don't apply Vaseline right before you have sex because it really isn't a good sexual lubricant, particularly since it can cause the latex that is used in condoms to weaken and break. Also, if you have oral sex, women can taste it and again tend to not like what they taste. On the same note, I've also heard women complain about men who used lotions, talcum powder, and cologne on or near the penis. Before you start using anything on your genitals, check with your partner.

The penis in general is not susceptible to a huge number of serious medical conditions; however, there are a few conditions you should be aware of. The first is *priapism*. This word describes an erection that won't go down. This might sound like nothing to worry about. In fact, it might sound like all your wishes just came true, but it's actually dangerous and it's often painful. Priapism is significantly more complicated than a really hard erection that lasts a long time, and it needs immediate medical attention. Priapism occurs if you are finished having sex and your erection won't go down, no matter what you do or how many cold showers you take. It's as though your penis is stuck in the "on" position. If this happens, you need to get medical help or you risk permanent damage to your erectile tissue. Priapism is fairly rare. Nonetheless, you should know about it. Primary causes of priapism are trauma, alcohol or drug abuse, head injury, and some medications.

Another unusual condition is called *Peyronie's disease*. Most men's penises aren't completely straight. They may curve a bit to one side or point up or down. This is normal. However, if your penis looks like it's curving more in one direction than it used to, you might have a problem called Peyronie's disease. This comes about because of scar tissue developing on one side of the penis; this shortens that side. This can be caused by injury to the penis or sometimes it just occurs for no apparent reason. If you think your penis is developing a curve, take Polaroids of it while it's erect and keep track of whether there really is a change over a few months. If so, take the pictures to your doctor for a consultation and find out whether you need to do something to

correct it before it gets so serious that it's starting to take a U-turn.
This condition is correctable with surgery.

Speaking of injury to the penis, even though the penis doesn't
have a bone in it, you can still fracture your erectile tissue. Here's
how this is most likely to happen. You and your partner have had a
few drinks, and there you are, having sex in the rear entry position,
in and out, in and out. The room is dark, and you can't see much.
You're going pretty fast, and you're really getting some good strokes
in. You're going all the way in and all the way out, and then, on an in
stroke, you miss your partner's vagina and hit her hip instead. You
hear a cracking sound, you're in incredible pain, and a bruise
appears that covers most of your penis.

It will probably heal within a few days, but if this happens to
you, err on the side of caution and see a doctor. Here's a safe sex
rule: Never operate heavy equipment while under the influence of
alcohol.

PENIS RULE # 4: Creative shaving can give the illusion of size.

One of the things I can recommend to alter the appearance of the
penis and make it look longer is creative shaving. In short, maybe
your penis looks small because it's hidden by your pubic hair. A little
shaving can give the illusion of a longer penis.

Here's how to shave the hair on and around your genitals: You can
use either a regular razor with soap or shaving gel, or a beard trimmer.
(I believe an electric beard trimmer works best.) Obviously, be very
careful as you shave in this area. Shave all the hair off your scrotum
and trim all of the hair off the shaft of your penis. Trim the tufts of hair
between your thighs and your scrotum with scissors and then shave
this area. Now, here's the illusion part. Stand in front of a mirror and

look at your penis when it isn't erect. Shave about a square inch above your penis. This will make it look longer. Then, use the beard trimmer to skim across your remaining pubic hair so that they're all about half an inch long. Shaved or trimmed pubic hair is a trend which I hope continues. It makes oral sex so much better (more about this in Chapter Five). The only problem with shaving pubic hairs is that you have to keep doing it daily. If you don't like the appearance of the shaved area and decide to let it grow back, be prepared for a few days of itching. This can usually be relieved with talcum powder.

Other hair-removal options include electrolysis or laser hair removal. Laser hair removal may take three or four sessions in order to completely remove hair from your genital area, but the results are generally very good.

PENIS RULE # 5: Your penis reacts to emotional *and* physical stimuli.

Years ago, I met a man named Frank who complained about erectile dysfunction. No matter what his wife did to his penis, Frank couldn't get an erection. When Frank and his wife first met, he was incredibly attracted to her. She was both beautiful and exciting. So he proposed. Unfortunately, he and his wife didn't get along so well. In fact, they fought about everything, from politics and religion to how to park the car. As you might imagine, his failure to get erect created some additional problems for an already troubled relationship. His wife was convinced that there was nothing wrong with him sexually. She said, "I know that what's wrong with him is that he is angry at me. Until he gets over that anger, he's not going to get hard." He said, "Don't be ridiculous." And he tried all kinds of solutions: he consulted with psychiatrists, and he consulted with sex therapists, and he took herbs and pills. But nothing worked. After a year or so of this, the couple divorced. Frank met a woman he liked; they started dating; he told her about his problem; she said, "Well, let's just cuddle and see what happens." After a couple of weeks of cuddling, lo and behold, Frank was erect. It was a miracle! "Whatever I had, I'm cured," Frank said. He took this statement one step further: "Now that I'm cured," he announced, "I can reconcile with my ex-wife and show her that I don't have any sexual problems!" And that's what he did. You won't be surprised to hear that once again, he couldn't get an erection.

"Well," he said. "I guess my penis has a mind of its own."

My response to him is: "No, your penis does not have a mind of its own. But it is connected to your mind, your emotions, your thoughts, your feelings, as well as to your body. Pay attention!"

I once spoke to another man who played tennis every Saturday afternoon in the summer for at least two hours and then dragged himself home, exhausted and at least a little dehydrated, to make love to his girlfriend. "Why," he asked, "am I not fully erect?"

If you are worried, tired, or stressed, this is going to have an impact on your erection. Many men are in complete denial about this. They try to have sex under horrible conditions—when they are drunk, tired, hungry, or upset. They start having intercourse and then when it isn't really happening, they start flogging their penis, or berating it, or trying to have sex faster. The likelihood of any of these methods working is minimal. If you experience an erection problem, and you've checked yourself out medically, it may be a sign that you should look at yourself and ask yourself what is going on in your life. There may be something you need at that point more than you need sex.

Here's my advice: It's wise to pay attention to your penis: it may be telling you something you need to know!

chapter two

POWER TO THE PENIS!

The typical man starts out approaching sex with a "doing what comes naturally" attitude. He may have good instincts and things may turn out pretty much all right. Nonetheless, no matter how many partners he has or how much he may enjoy sex, he is still always a little unsure of what is going to happen next. Even if sex works out 99 percent of the time, and it usually does, most of the time he doesn't feel totally in control; it is his penis that is charge of the situation.

In order to be a really great and self-assured lover, you need a little bit more than nature and instincts. You have to know that you are in control of your penis instead of the other way around. The two qualities that a man needs in bed are self-confidence and control. If you pay attention and follow the instructions in this chapter, not only will you be in charge of your penis, you will have a degree of sexual mastery that you probably didn't believe possible.

Much of this book is geared to giving advice to men about how to please a woman sexually. This chapter is a little different because it is specifically directed at a man's sexual pleasure and satisfaction. Yes, if you follow this advice, your sexual partner will benefit greatly, but this chapter is for *you*, the male reader. The information comes from my experience of more than twenty years, working with men to improve their sexual skills and pleasure.

Few men ever develop the level of sexual control and confidence that they really want. That's why I'm going to share some of the secrets that can bring men to a more advanced level of lovemaking. I don't want to sound like an infomercial here, but there is a whole world of sexuality available to you if you are willing to take the time. I want you to be aware of the things you can do with your penis. I want you to be aware of the levels of pleasure you are capable of feeling. That's why I'm going to give you some information that will put you in total charge of your penis.

PENIS RULE #6: Exercising your penis is guaranteed to give you greater sexual skills.

The following exercises are designed to help you be fully aware of your penis, your erection, your arousal, your orgasm, and your ejaculation. This awareness will ultimately translate into skill. Doing these exercises even a little bit can't help but increase your sexual confidence and pleasure. If you want to develop really advanced sexual expertise, this is how you can open the door to incredible sexual mastery and unlock the secrets of male multiple orgasm. Anyone who has ever learned how to flex a muscle can do these exercises. Learning them is a little like a riding a bicycle. At first you may wobble and teeter and fall, but eventually you're able to put the whole thing about pedaling and balance together.

BREATHING RIGHT HELPS YOU BECOME A GREAT LOVER

Like everything else in life, great sex starts with breathing. Having said that, I bet I can anticipate that your first question is: *What do breathing exercises have to do with sex?* Here's the answer.

You can't learn how to be in control of your penis until you are able to slow down enough so that you can be aware of what is happening in your entire body, including your penis. The one quality that really fabulous lovers have in common is awareness. They are able to slow down and be deliberate in their actions. When a really great lover touches a woman's skin, yes, it feels good to her, but it also feels good to him; his partner can sense his excitement. That's because he's not rushing; he's not hurried; he's not racing to have an orgasm and be done with sex. He's enjoying what he is doing in the moment, and he's able to experience and convey pleasure. Awareness is also what helps a man sense his partner's body; it helps him know what to do.

Breathing exercises will help you slow down and increase awareness. Breathing exercises are going to help you feel what happens as you become aroused. Eventually, I want you to be able to feel the difference between orgasm and ejaculation, and I want you to be aware of the different phases of ejaculation. Being able to do this is what's going to give you sexual control. And it all starts with breathing.

Did you know that it is almost impossible to get an erection when you are holding your breath? Knowing more about breathing will definitely enhance your skills as a lover. It's that simple. So don't get nervous because the first exercise in this book is about breathing. This is not impractical or ethereal advice. Breathing exercises will also help give you confidence and control. Some of the most successful sports teams in the country do breathing and meditation exercises. The coaches know that it increases focus, relaxation, and concentration. Learning more about how to breathe during sex will also increase your pleasure.

You can use your breath to relax. You can use your breath to bring you back to the moment. You can use your breath to help you concentrate on your pleasure and on your partner's pleasure. You can use your breath to help you become aroused; you can use your breath to increase the physical sensations in your genitals. These are just some of the ways your breath can help you improve your sex life. Here are some simple breathing exercises to help put you more in touch with your sexuality.

breathing exercise # one

Start by sitting down and getting comfortable. Now breathe in and out slowly through your nostrils. Relax. Let your shoulders drop. Feel the tension leaving your body. Feel yourself becoming more centered. As you are doing this, count your breaths.

On the in breath, count one.

On the out breath, count two.

Continue breathing in and breathing out.

Do this to the count of ten.

This is the most basic meditation breath exercise. Let your breath help you relax and get centered. Whenever you are feeling tense, use your breath to relax. Let your breath help you enjoy sex by keeping you more connected to the experience. Let your breath help you become more aware of your own body and of your partner's body.

breathing exercise # two

Sit upright with a straight spine. You can do this in a chair or sitting cross-legged on the floor. Relax and get centered.

Start breathing through your nose. Take slow, deep breaths.

Take three slow, deep breaths in and out through your nostrils.

As you breathe, visualize your breath going through your body.

Feel your breath going down through your chest, through your stomach, through your lower abdomen, and all the way down to your genitals. Visualize your breath going all the way down to your scrotum and then back up your body and out through your nose. Do this for five to ten minutes. Do you feel the sensation of energy flowing into your genitals? Before you have sex, try a little bit of this deep breathing. Let it help bring energy and focus to your penis.

MASTURBATION CAN TEACH YOU HOW TO MAKE LOVE TO A WOMAN

PENIS RULE # 7: Don't fall for all those old myths about masturbation.

For something that is so much fun, masturbation still has a bad reputation. Masturbation is not bad for you in any way. In fact, it's been shown to help people learn about their sexual response, cure sexual problems, and increase self-esteem. Forget the stories from great-grandpa's day about hairy palms and insanity. The only time masturbation becomes a problem is if it becomes compulsive. This means that you're masturbating because you get incredibly anxious if you don't. When this happens you are no longer masturbating for the sake of pleasure.

Some men work themselves up into a compulsive masturbation habit where they are masturbating every hour on the hour. It's not how often you masturbate that's the problem; it's whether you have control of your behavior or if the behavior is controlling you.

Some men believe that once you are in a sexual relationship with a partner, you are supposed to give up masturbation; they sometimes also think that they shouldn't even want to masturbate. This feeling corresponds with the way many women feel upset and insulted if they discover that their partners are masturbating. For the record: you can be in a terrific relationship and still want to masturbate. The majority of men like to masturbate no matter what their life situation. And, just so we include everybody, there are also some men who rarely, if ever, masturbate. It simply doesn't feel that good to them. Both attitudes are normal.

Masturbation can be thought of as a learning tool on the path to becoming the best lover. When I was a surrogate partner, I watched hundreds of men masturbate, mostly to see if they were doing anything that was inadvertently getting in the way of their sexual enjoyment. I would always start out by telling them to pretend that I wasn't there and to masturbate the same way they would if they were by themselves. What I saw amazed me. Here are the things that surprised me the most:

- How short a time it took
- All the roughhousing and manhandling those men subject themselves to. (Who taught them to do that?)
- There are many men who treat their penis as though they hate it.

- There seems to be this belief that the faster and firmer you do it, the better.
- There also seems to be this belief that if you have trouble reaching an orgasm, you should just work harder and stroke faster.

some information on penile sensitivity

Sex therapists typically spend a great deal of time teaching people about touch. We teach them how to touch each other, and we teach them how to touch themselves. Self-touch is a powerful tool in acquiring the skills necessary for sexual mastery, but you're going to have to become more conscious and deliberate about the way you touch your penis when you masturbate. I want you to learn how to masturbate in such a way that you are totally aware of what you are doing and what you are feeling. I want you to be aware of every centimeter of skin on your penis, and I want you to be aware of every sensation that you are experiencing in your hands and your fingers as you stroke your penis.

If you were to visit a sexual therapist as a client, chances are that one of the first things you would learn is something called *sensate focus*. This is a technique that therapists use to help make people more aware of what they are feeling as they are feeling it. We're going to talk more about this in the chapter on touch between partners, but for our purposes here, I want you to start thinking about sensate focus as you masturbate. This means that you learn to be aware not only of the sensations in your genitals, but also of what you are feeling in your hands and fingers. They are also filled with sensitive nerve endings.

I've helped many men develop superior lovemaking skills, and I know that it is wrong, wrong, wrong to beat your penis up. In fact, if you use a masturbation stroke that is too firm or fast, you can end up losing some sensitivity in your penis. The end result is that you may not be able to feel and enjoy a lover's more sensitive touch. Women tend to be confused when they are with a man who gives them instructions of the "use your hand and squeeze tighter" variety. Some men actually lose so much sensation that it is almost as though their penises have forgotten how to enjoy the feeling inside a vagina, sometimes making them think that intercourse alone doesn't give them the stimulation they need to reach orgasm.

Another issue that will impact you as a lover is how long you spend masturbating. Obviously, there is no right or wrong here. However, if you masturbate for a long time (thirty minutes or more) before ejaculation, you may discover that this is another practice that will reduce the sensitivity of your penis. In my research, I have personally found that men who masturbate between ten and fifteen minutes before ejaculating tend to have the highest levels of penile sensitivity.

Very frequent masturbation can also contribute to a penis that is less sensitive. This is not true for all men, but if you feel that your penis is less sensitive than it used to be, you can try cutting down on how many times you masturbate. Start by keeping track of how often you masturbate. Then start cutting back gradually—about 10 percent a week. Continue doing this until you begin to notice a difference in both the level of your sensitivity and the ease and pleasure with which you ejaculate.

An additional method for improving penile sensitivity is to change how you stroke your penis during masturbation. Try slowing down your stroke so that you are moving at a different, more relaxed pace. See if you can slow it down 50 percent every time you masturbate until your stroke becomes more of a caress. If your penis doesn't seem to stay aroused with this technique, alternate your old, faster and firmer stroke with a new slower, more delicate stroke. After you have been doing this for a while, see if you can gradually switch completely to the slower method. Eventually, your penis will become more sensitive and accustomed to this more sensual method.

You can also increase your penile sensitivity by switching to masturbatory methods that simulate being inside a woman's vagina. The simplest way of doing this is to use a lot of lubrication and masturbate with one hand held over the head of the penis. I've heard a lot of other creative ideas about how to simulate the soft, warm, and wet sensation of a vagina. Some of these include putting a soft sock into the clothes dryer and filling it with lubrication, or filling a reusable lambskin condom with a water-based lubricant. Most adult shops also have an interesting supply of artificial vaginas.

THE PC MUSCLE: YOUR MOST IMPORTANT SEXUAL TOOL

If you want to be a really great lover, you need to start exercising your PC muscle. Remember that both men and women have a muscle located at the base of the trunk of the body, right near the genitals. The pubococcygeus (PC) muscle is the muscle that contracts when you ejaculate; it's also the muscle you use to stop urine flow. Your PC muscle may be your most important and essential sexual tool. Getting more control over your PC muscle will give you sexual mastery and bring you to a new level of lovemaking skills. Strengthening this muscle can also help you make your orgasm stronger and more exciting. From a purely health-oriented point of view, it may also help prevent future prostate problems.

finding your PC muscle

Reach under your testicles with two fingers and touch yourself lightly. Think about what you do when you are urinating and want to stop the flow by tightening a muscle. Tighten that muscle now. That is the PC muscle. When you tighten it, you may notice that your penis and testicles also move slightly.

Here are some exercises to strengthen your PC muscle. Doing them daily could be the best sexual advice you ever receive. The great thing about PC exercises is that you can do them just about any time and any place. Do them every morning in the shower, do them when you're watching television, do them before you go to sleep. You can even do them at your desk.

This exercise is so easy that you may think you can ignore it. Don't do that. Being in control of your PC muscle will inevitably give you greater lovemaking skills than you can possibly imagine.

PC muscle exercise

Start this exercise by getting comfortable wherever you are. Breathe in and out through your nostrils a few times just to get relaxed. The first few times you do this exercise, you may want to place your fingers on your PC muscle just to make sure that you're working the right muscles.

Now flex your PC muscle and hold it for two seconds.

Then release and relax.

This is such a simple exercise for such a big payoff!

Keep breathing naturally as you do this exercise. **Do not hold your breath** as you tense the muscle.

The most common error men make when doing this PC exercise is to overdo it. The PC muscle can become sore. I want you to build it up gradually. I also want you to make sure that you experience the sensation of relaxing the muscle as well as tensing it. Slow and steady is the way to go.

Another common error men make is to squeeze other muscles instead of or along with the PC. The PC is not connected to your butt, stomach, thighs, etc. Try to keep these other muscles groups relaxed. They will probably want to join in, but see if you can keep them separate and really isolate the PC in and of itself.

At first, I want you to do 25 repetitions of this exercise once a day. After a few days, do 25 reps 2 times a day. In six days, increase to 25 reps 3 times a day.

advanced PC muscle exercise

At the end of the first week of doing PC exercises, you should be ready to move on to advanced PC muscle exercises. Here's how you do them:

Tighten the PC muscle to the count of 5. Hold this for a count of 5. Then push it back out to a count of 5. Start by doing 5 reps a day. At the end of the third day, increase to 10.

> **IMPORTANT: Your PC muscle is the foundation for all of the other exercises in this chapter. You will not be able to do the rest of them successfully until this muscle is toned and in shape.**

DEVELOPING GREATER AWARENESS OF WHAT YOUR PENIS IS FEELING

There are many elements involved in being a great lover. You have to learn to use your head and your heart, as well as your body. But from the point of view of pure physical technique, the first step on the path to being a great lover revolves around your becoming more conscious and aware of what your penis is feeling.

Arousal awareness is a very important part of building advanced sexual skills. Some men have sex or masturbate with so much intensity that they have no sense whatsoever of the different levels of arousal. Before you can learn to control your penis and your ejaculation, you need to be aware of what you are feeling as you are feeling it. The following exercises are designed to put men more in touch with what they experience from the moment they start to become aroused to the time they reach orgasm and ejaculation.

These exercises help you gain confidence and put you in control of your level of arousal. They give you greater awareness of the peaks and valleys of sexual excitement; they teach you a great deal of what you need to know about your penis and its sexual response. Peaking exercises will help you heighten your excitement and also increase your staying power as a lover.

sexual skill exercise # one: arousal awareness

Before you start doing this masturbation exercise, you need to think a bit about how you become aroused and how that arousal increases.

It's easier to describe your arousal level to yourself if you assign number values to your different levels of arousal. I use the numbers 1–10. Remember that these numbers are not about how hard or soft your penis is. We are talking about what your penis is feeling, not what it's doing, so don't make the mistake of using the numbers to describe your erection.

For example, when you first begin stroking your genitals, you may be at an arousal level of #1. Then, as you become more excited, this number will go up. Assign #10 to the point of actual orgasm. In between, you will go through the rest of the numbers. At #2, you will begin to experience genital sensations; at #3, these sensations are getting stronger. At #4–6, you get more and more excited. By #7–8, you are fully aroused and it would be very difficult to stop. Level #9 is the point of no return; you feel as though you have to continue to orgasm. Level #10 is orgasm itself.

The first time you do this exercise, all I want you to do is to become much more aware of your own levels and feelings of excitement and arousal. With this in mind, start caressing your genitals slowly. Follow your feeling of excitement as it progresses from arousal level #1 through arousal levels #7 or #8. Notice what your body is doing. Be aware of the difference in your breathing; notice how your muscles and skin feel; notice the buildup of sexual tension. Don't stop caressing yourself, but every few minutes, as your excitement increases, ask yourself, "What is my current level of arousal?" Focus on what you are doing to yourself to become more aroused. Feel the sensations in your hands and fingers. Be aware of where you are touching. At level #9, notice how your body is propelling forward to orgasm; feel yourself cross over to level #10, and be aware of exactly what you are experiencing.

sexual skill exercise # two: peaking

This time you will do the same exercise, but with a sophisticated difference. You will be learning how to slowly increase your level of arousal to a peak, hence the name "peaking," and then bring yourself back to the previous level. This exercise is called "peaking" because it will put you more closely in touch with your various levels or peaks of excitement. Eventually, it will help you reach a point where you are able to allow your arousal to peak and subside as you wish. After you have done this exercise several times, you will begin to see for yourself what I mean when I talk about getting a sense of sexual control. This exercise is going to help put you in charge of your penis instead of the other way around.

Begin stroking and caressing your genitals and bring yourself to what would be about level #2 or #3. At this point, either slow down or stop the caressing and let your body go back to level #1. Then resume your touching and bring yourself much further along on your way to orgasm. Go to about level #5 on your arousal scale. Stop or slow down again, and let your excitement go back down to about level #3. Do this several times. Each time, allow yourself a couple of minutes at each level, both the highs and the lows. Bring yourself to level #7 or #8. Allow your arousal to subside, and then bring it up again. How close to level #8 can you get and still stop? After about twenty minutes of working on this exercise, you can move forward to orgasm.

Do this exercise several times a week, about twenty minutes each time. Take your time doing it. You may become so aroused that you will want to jump forward to level #10, but you'll be losing the benefit of what you're doing so try to stick with it.

This exercise puts you in touch with how your penis works. I can't recommend it enough as a way to give you greater confidence in both your penis and your lovemaking abilities. There is an added advantage to this exercise: many men say that allowing their level of arousal to build and subside in this way ultimately makes for a stronger orgasm.

THE PC MUSCLE AND PEAKING

In the earlier peaking exercise, you learned how to differentiate among the different levels of sexual arousal. Now we are going to combine that awareness with what we have learned about the PC muscle. One of the wonderful things the PC muscle can help you do is to slow down your arousal. This is one of the ways you can increase staying time and be in control of your penis. In this instance, the PC muscle is being used almost as a brake.

There are different kinds of PC muscle squeezes. Start by knowing about all of them. A man might give the PC muscle one long hard squeeze, or he might do two medium squeezes, or a series of several quick squeezes all in a row.

Try this and make sure that you can do all these different types of squeezes.

You are going to need to experiment for yourself to see how this works with your body. When you are aroused, obviously you don't want to bring your arousal down so far that you lose your erection. Only you can do the kind of experimentation with your body to know what works for you. If you give your PC muscle a couple of short squeezes, will this do the job, or do you need longer, harder squeezes?

When experimenting with your PC muscle, you need to be aware that if you squeeze it too much or too hard before you are fully erect, you could lose the erection.

Learn exactly how much or how little pressure you need to exert on your PC muscle by doing the following peaking exercise. The PC muscle is the key to male multiple orgasm. Knowing how to use it gives you a powerful skill that you can rely on. Let's say, for example, that you are making love and you are so super-aroused that you are having trouble getting control just by peaking. So you use the PC muscle to help you.

sexual skill exercise # three: braking the PC muscle

Allow yourself twenty minutes of slow caresses to your penis, gradually peaking through the various levels starting with level #3. In this exercise, as you peak at each of these levels, you will be using your PC muscle as a "brake" on your penis. As your arousal builds, be aware of the level you have reached and name it to yourself: Level #2 starting to get sensations in my penis. Level #3, the sensations are getting stronger. Now peak at level #3 and squeeze your PC muscle. Do you feel your arousal drop a level? Continue masturbating and bring your arousal to a more excited level #4. Now squeeze your PC level and watch your arousal drop. Continue doing this one level at a time and at each peak, squeeze your PC muscle and be aware of the effect it has on your penis. Continue on with this exercise. Can you go to a fully aroused and excited level #8 and use your PC muscle to put a brake on your arousal? Can you go to level #9 and peak? As you do this exercise, experiment to learn which method of squeezing can bring your arousal down a level without making you lose your erection. See if you can go all the way through all the levels up to #9, peaking just before you reach the point of no return.

The PC muscle is an incredible sexual tool. Here are some important points to keep in mind about your PC.

- Tightening your PC muscle when you are having sex is one technique that can help you last longer.

- If you are a man who has difficulty ejaculating or reaching orgasm, don't squeeze your PC muscles when you are aroused. Instead, you have to keep checking yourself to make sure that your PC muscle stays relaxed.

THE SECRET TO MALE MULTIPLE ORGASM

Both men and women find it difficult to believe that a man can be multi-orgasmic. They think it's some kind of myth, but it's not. A few years back, I wrote a book called *How to Make Love All Night*. It's all about how a man can become multi-orgasmic, and when it came out, I still remember the disbelief expressed in some of the questions I was asked on talk shows. However, I know that multiple orgasms really are within the realm of possibility for most men. It's impossible to cover all the information about male multiple orgasm in this one chapter, but learning about it will give you some background to get started.

Most of us think that after an orgasm, a man's body and his penis need a chance to recover. It's true that some men, particularly when they are young, are able to rest for a short period of time and then have another erection, and then continue to do this for an extended period of time. That's not what I mean by multi-orgasmic. The multi-orgasmic man is able to experience all the sensations and pleasures of orgasm without losing his erection, and he can experience these sensations again and again until he chooses to stop. All you need in order to start down the path of becoming this kind of lover is information and motivation.

Here's some of what you need to know:

Most people think that in a man, orgasm and ejaculation are the same thing. **This is not true.** Ejaculation occurs when the PC muscle spasms and forces semen out of the penis. It is a localized genital response. You can have an ejaculation without an orgasm, and many men have experienced this sensation at least once. They ejaculate and they feel the release of tension, but most of the pleasure of orgasm is missing. When this occurs, men tend to wonder, "What happened?!" Here's the explanation: Ejaculation is a localized genital response. Orgasm is a full-body response. It includes muscle spasms, rapid heart rate, and all those intense and wonderful sensations of pleasure. Orgasm includes a physical sense of relief, release, and intense pleasure.

So what is male multiple orgasm? When a man becomes more aware of his body and takes the time to do the necessary exercises, he can learn how to experience orgasm while holding back on his ejaculations. That means that he can have more than one orgasm (sometimes several) without ejaculation. He can have an orgasm and continue making love—without losing his erection!

In order to have multiple orgasms, you need to recognize and acknowledge that orgasm and ejaculation can occur separately, and that orgasm without ejaculation can feel as good as (or better than) an orgasm with ejaculation.

UNDERSTANDING AND CONTROLLING EJACULATION

When most men reach a level #9 and what feels like the point of inevitability as far as ejaculation is concerned, whether they are masturbating or having sex with a partner, they typically continue thrusting and moving toward ejaculation. This body movement contributes to the fact that all the sensations of orgasm and ejaculation get mixed together and it's difficult to separate exactly what you are experiencing as it happens.

The act of ejaculation actually has two separate phases: emission and expulsion. *Emission* is when the semen moves from the testicles to an area near the prostate. *Expulsion* is when the PC muscle spasms and forces semen out of your penis.

You should be able to feel these two distinct phases. Here's a peaking exercise to help you be more aware of what your ejaculation feels like.

sexual skill exercise # four: ejaculation awareness

Now that you are more in touch with your arousal levels and have greater arousal control, it's time for you to become more aware of what happens to your body as you ejaculate. This exercise is going to help you be conscious of the two phases of ejaculation: emission and expulsion.

Once again, you start out by masturbating and stroking your penis slowly. As you did before, be aware of each level of arousal. At each level, peak and let your arousal go down a level before you start again. When you reach level #9 and hit the point of inevitability where you know you are going to ejaculate, **stop** the stimulation. For the purposes of this exercise, do not use the PC muscle to inhibit your ejaculation. **Don't thrust.** Just hold still and concentrate on your genital area. In this instance, **concentration** is the key word. When you do this, you should be able to feel the two different phases of ejaculation. You will be able to feel the semen start to move and then about two seconds later, you will feel the PC muscle contract.

sexual skill exercise # five: male multiple orgasm

Start this as you did the other peaking exercises. Bring your arousal up through levels #3, #4, and #5. At each level, let your arousal subside before bringing it back up. Do this until you reach level #9. Don't use the PC muscle yet because we are saving it for its big moment, its starring role, when it is going to help you have multiple orgasms. Masturbate as you have done before, letting your arousal build to a peak, then let it subside before moving to a higher level.

Just continue forward until you reach the point of inevitability— that place where you are sure you are about to ejaculate. Then, in that nanosecond when you hit that point of no return, slam on your brakes and squeeze your PC muscle as hard as you can for about ten seconds. **Open your eyes wide**, take deep breaths, and continue thrusting or stroking your penis. It's important to note here that most men close their eyes as they approach orgasm. This technique will only work if you go against your instincts and open your eyes.

What should happen at this point is that you feel all the sensations of an orgasm without the ejaculation. When a man first starts doing this, he may experience only a partial, instead of a full, orgasm. Your heart will be pounding and your muscles contracting. You may need to slow down and let your arousal drop a couple of levels, but don't stop totally because you don't want to lose your erection. The important thing is that you should still have an erection and be able to continue. This time, as you let your arousal levels rise, don't stop yourself. Just continue on to orgasm and ejaculation.

THREE WEEKS TO MALE MULTIPLE ORGASM

Most men can begin to master the fundaments of multiple orgasm in three to four weeks. You will be using the exercises in this chapter so read through them again. When you're ready to experience the phenomenon of male multiple orgasm firsthand (no pun intended), here's a program you can follow. If you want to extend this program for another week or more, you can certainly do so. Do all the daily breathing and PC exercises as outlined, but allow longer before the awareness and peaking exercises.

Week One

Day 1–7	Breathing Exercise # One	1–5 minutes
	Breathing Exercise # Two	5–10 minutes
Day 1–3	PC Muscle Exercise	25 reps 1x daily
Day 4–5	PC Muscle Exercise	25 reps 2x daily
Day 6–7	PC Muscle Exercise	25 reps 3x daily

Week Two

Day 1–7	Breathing Exercise # One	1–5 minutes
	Breathing Exercise # Two	5–10 minutes
	PC Muscle Exercise	25 reps 3x daily
Day 1–3	Advanced PC Muscle Exercise	5 reps daily
Day 4–7	Advanced PC Muscle Exercise	10 reps daily
Day 1	Sexual Skill Exercise # One: Arousal Awareness	
Day 3 or 4	Sexual Skill Exercise # Two: Peaking	
Day 5 or 7	Sexual Skill Exercise # Three: Braking the PC Muscle	

Week Three

Day 1–7	Breathing Exercise # One	5 minutes
	Breathing Exercise # Two	5–10 minutes
	Advanced PC Muscle Exercise	20 reps 3x daily
Day 1 or 2	Sexual Skill Exercise # Three: Braking the PC Muscle	
Day 3 or 4	Sexual Skill Exercise # Four: Ejaculation Awareness	
Day 6 or 7	Sexual Skill Exercise # Five: Male Multiple Orgasm	

Men should keep up the breathing and PC muscle exercises every day for life. It's also a good idea to do a peaking exercise with awareness of emission and expulsion or a male multiple orgasm exercise once every week or two in addition to having sex with your partner. If you have a latent ability to have multiple orgasms, the above schedule should bring it out within three to four weeks.

A WORD ON SEX WITH A PARTNER

In this chapter, we've focused a good deal on masturbation as an exercise. What you are doing here is training your body to respond in a certain way. It's a little like practicing your forehand, backhand, and serves before you play tennis with a partner.

There is no reason, however, why the peaking and arousal exercises cannot be done with a partner; if you have a partner who would enjoy practicing with you, by all means do so. The only hesitation I have in introducing a partner in this preliminary work is that it may put additional performance pressure on both of you. If you don't succeed immediately with a partner, you may be reluctant to try again, and she may also begin to feel anxious and pressured. You could end up having too many conversations of the "What-do-you-think-went-wrong?" variety.

Once your PC muscle has been trained and is in good shape, it will automatically respond in the peaking pattern when you are with a partner.

chapter three

TOUCHING HER *EVERYWHERE*

I recently met a man (let's call him Joe) who told me that he has a real problem with women, and he can't understand what's going wrong. Joe, who is in his late twenties, likes women; in fact, he loves women. He wants to spend time with women, and he wants to please them sexually. Joe is attractive enough, and many women like him when they first meet him, but after a couple of dates, almost every woman he meets doesn't want to go out with him again. He's asked a couple of them to explain what happened, and they both said something along the lines of, "It just wasn't happening for me." What is Joe doing wrong? From my perspective, his problem can be stated in one sentence: He doesn't know how to touch a woman. And that involves much more than just knowing what to do with his hands.

Here's something every man needs to know: *Your lover wants you to touch her.* She wants to be touched by all parts of you. She wants to be touched by your thoughts, your emotions, and your hands. She wants to be touched by your words, and she wants to be touched by your eyes. The best lovers arouse their partners by using all parts of themselves.

FIRST STEPS FIRST

Some people assume that when a man and a woman are attracted to each other, they will immediately find a place to be alone, rip off their clothes, and jump each other's bones. Well, sometimes it happens that way, but it often doesn't; sexual relationships don't always proceed smoothly. Sometimes those first awkward moments never get fixed, and consequently the sexual relationship rests on a base of clumsy habits and insecurities. What happens then is that two people who may really like each other never get to explore their sexuality together.

As a sex educator, I would like to change that. When I talk about how to initiate touch and the first stages of a sexual relationship, I don't mean to sound like a decorous nineteenth-century maiden, because everyone knows this couldn't be further from the truth. However, from my own experience as a teacher and consultant, I know that most people are a little confused and uncertain about how to move a potentially great sexual relationship from point A to point B and beyond.

So exactly when do you touch a woman? How soon after you meet her can you reach out to hold or stroke her hand? What about a woman you already know? Is she always receptive? The best lovers try to be aware of how a woman is feeling. For example, if she is sitting on the couch talking to her best friend while she is giving herself a pedicure, is that a good time to initiate sex? Probably not!

The one thing you must do before you begin to touch a woman is to assess her mental state. Can you tell what kind of mood she is in? Can you tell how she feels about you? Stop, take a minute, and think about these questions. For a new partner you haven't had sex with yet, this means being able to read the nonverbal cues that tell you whether she likes you enough to want you to touch her. For a partner you've had sex with many, many times, this means being able to assess her emotional state and stress level to figure out what, if any, kind of touch she would welcome. Is this the right moment for an affectionate and supportive kiss on the top of the head? Or is it the right moment for a steamy embrace?

One woman I know filed for divorce because her husband always seemed to be so out of touch with what she was feeling sexually. She said that if she put on her most revealing lingerie and stuck her breasts in his face, he would be far more likely to reach for the television remote than her body. On the other hand, whenever she was sitting in front of the computer in the middle of an important work assignment, he invariably decided that this was exactly the right moment to express all his sexual fantasies. Was he simply oblivious to his partner's messages or was he being purposefully perverse? Who knows? But they are no longer together.

Touch is one part of what we call nonverbal communication or body language. Many books have been written on how to assess another person's body language as well as how to use your own body language to attract partners. Some of these books are quite good, but many others are terrible, filled with cheap, cheesy gimmicks that don't even work. Small wonder that so many guys remain mystified about the messages a woman might be using her body to convey.

As most of us realize, there are two forms of communication: verbal and nonverbal. Verbal communication is the content of what we say and includes the actual words we use. Nonverbal communication (or body language) includes everything else. Think about how people convey their emotions without speaking, simply by the way they move their bodies. Do you sometimes communicate with your hands, for example? How about your eyes? There are people whose eyes are so expressive that when you look into them, you can almost feel what they feel. Other ways of communicating nonverbally include arm and leg movements, posture, facial expressions, and touch. When we speak, we are actually using both verbal and nonverbal communication. The verbal part is the content of what we say, while the nonverbal part, which includes voice tone as well as facial expression and body language, is typically how we express our emotions.

Some people are geniuses at conveying their emotional state to others even without words. Others are terrible at it. Conversely, there are also people who can quickly get a read on what another person is feeling from nonverbal behavior alone, while others always seem to remain clueless. In general, women have a slight edge over men in being able to send and receive emotional communications accurately through body language. It's very educational for a man to learn more about nonverbal communication. Men who are adept at expressing their emotions nonverbally are usually very successful in their relationships with women, as are men who are perceptive enough to be able to hear what women's bodies are telling them. Nonverbal skills are an important part of one's charisma and likeability as well as attractiveness.

In the study of nonverbal behavior, any body part you use to send a message is called a *channel*. A channel can be very specific, like the eyes, or it could contain multiple sources of emotional information such as the entire face. Verbal communication is more conscious and straightforward, relying on a single channel to convey meaning.

Nonverbal communication, involving numerous channels that are mostly unconscious, is amazingly complex and varied. Whether we're aware of it or not, we are always interpreting the nonverbal messages we receive from others.

Although touch is just one form of nonverbal communication, it's incredibly important in romantic and sexual relationships and can be used as a measure of the level of intimacy that exists between two people. As far as touch is concerned, we all have boundaries about how and where we want to be touched. I have a friend who is uncomfortable being touched, even on the hand, by anyone but her husband; as far as he's concerned, however, she says he can put his hands anywhere he wants. He has gotten past all of her boundaries.

Men who want to be successful with women would be well served if they spent time learning how to both express and translate non-verbal signals. I'm friendly with a thirty-something-year-old guy who I met when he was still in his twenties. At that time, he had a major complaint about life: he was having trouble meeting and con-necting with women. He didn't want to get into a relationship at that time. His goal was to have sex with a lot of women. When I met him, he'd had sex with only a handful of women, and a couple of those experiences were disastrous one-night stands. I decided to take him under my wing and give him some advice. He paid attention to what I taught him, and within the next couple of years, he'd had sex with maybe thirty-five women. The secret? The advice on nonverbal communication I'm about to give you.

I'm going to give you advice on how to tell if a woman is interested in being touched. I want you to know how to touch, kiss, and take off a woman's clothes; I want you to develop real expertise in caressing and stimulating a woman's genitals. When it comes to touch, there are three different kinds of situations to think about: a first impression; a first date; and a relationship in which you've already had sex.

THE FIRST MEETING AND THE FIRST TOUCH

Many women remember those special times when we had just met somebody new, and we were so attracted that we practically quivered in anticipation of that first touch. Almost inevitably, our eagerness had a great deal to do with anticipation. Most of us wanted to be touched not because a man acted like he wanted to grope us; no, we wanted to be touched because the man we were so attracted to was appropriately restrained and, consequently, nonthreatening. That allowed us to experience our sexual feelings without concern about being overwhelmed.

Since men still assume most of the responsibility for getting a relationship off the ground, it helps if you spend a little bit of time thinking about those first encounters and how to approach a woman you want to know better. In most real-life situations, the wrong touch in a first-impression situation can be a huge mistake, and here's why: In the language of those who study nonverbal communication, eye gaze and touch are called *intensifiers*. That means that eye gaze and touch will intensify (rather than change) whatever mood is already present in a social interaction.

For example, let's say that I walk into a party and a guy crosses the room and starts talking to me. For some reason, I take an instant dislike to him. It happens that way with some people. If he looks directly into my eyes while he's talking to me, I'm probably going to experience that as rude staring. It's going to intensify my already negative reactions. But if I was initially physically and emotionally attracted to this person, and he looked into my eyes, I would probably experience his gaze as positive and sexy.

It's the same thing with touch. If I'm in a crummy mood or don't really like or know a man, I don't want him to touch me. If he tries to put a hand on my knee, arm, or shoulder, I'll stiffen up, move away, or even cringe. If I'm feeling mellow or sort of attracted, I would probably enjoy that extra touch. If a man misreads a woman's signals and touches her prematurely or before she has the time or inclination to think about whether or not she was initially attracted to him, he might well blow his chances with her permanently.

If you are still kind of in the dark about how people use touch and gaze as intensifiers, it's time for you to do a little research. Be a psychologist for a day and start observing people's nonverbal behavior. Next time you go to a club or a party, try to put off your own agenda of connecting with a woman and, instead, start observing how couples interact. You can generally tell couples who are in love or who have recently had sex because they tend to gaze into each other's eyes and touch each other a lot. Use what you learn from your observations in your own life.

is she attracted to you?

Let's say you've just met an attractive woman at a party and you are standing next to her. The thing to do would be just to shake her hand. You sense a mutual attraction, and you would like to check out the possibilities by either touching her arm or asking for her phone number. How do you know whether or not she will be receptive to you? How do you know if she will find what you are doing offensive or forward?

Here are some signs that a woman might be interested in knowing you better:

- Are her eyes telling you something? Can you see if her pupils are dilated? The pupils in our eyes get bigger when we see something we like. (This happens even with babies.) Unfortunately, we can't always judge this accurately because we often meet potential romantic partners in darkened rooms, and even under ideal conditions, the change is small and hard to perceive. But you can notice whether her eyes widen in general when she looks at you. Is there a special sparkle or warmth?

- Is she letting you into her personal space? Does she stand close to you? Or if you try to move closer to her, does she move away? Personal space is our comfort zone. Just because she moves away doesn't necessarily mean she doesn't like you, but it does mean that she isn't yet comfortable letting you stand close to her. So don't push it. Many people, particularly women, start out being slightly guarded about personal space. Once they warm up, it can change considerably, but if you move too close too soon, it's more likely to create a freeze up than a warm up. Do any of you remember the *Seinfeld* episode that featured a man Jerry referred to as "a close talker"? Most of us are at least a little bit turned off by people who get too close and invade our space.

- Does *she* touch *you*? It's more socially acceptable and less threatening for a woman to touch a man she's just met in a social situation. If she reaches out to touch your arm or shoulder or hand, that's a message that she thinks she could like you, given half an opportunity. However, a casual touch is not an invitation, so don't get the wrong idea.

- Does she appear nervous or jittery? Is she clenching her hands or jiggling her leg? If so, she's probably not comfortable. Either something about the situation is making her uncomfortable or there is someplace else she would rather be.

- Does she look you directly in the eye, in a pleasant, non-staring way? Gazing directly at a man and then dropping your eyes is a universal sign of flirting. I've seen this done by babies as young as four months old. Eye contact is a very reliable barometer of a woman's responsiveness.

- Don't be confused by how much she smiles. Sure, smiling is a much better sign than frowning, but don't read too much into it. Women are trained socially to smile at everybody. It's almost automatic with us; I catch myself smiling at people I don't know and don't particularly want to know.

- If you move back just a small amount, does she inch closer to you or does she seem relieved?

GETTING PAST HELLO

Let's go to the next situation. You and a woman you are interested in have been out to dinner. You have taken her home and walked her to the door. Does she want you to touch her? Let's sum it up again. Is she looking into your eyes and do her eyes widen when she looks at you? Is she standing close to you and does she appear unhurried, as if she wants to linger? If so, she's probably giving you unspoken permission to touch her. Try a slight hug and see how she responds.

If she leans into you, you can hold her by the shoulders and kiss her forehead. How does she seem to be responding? Is her body language telling you that she'd like to see you again? Does her body language say that she would like to share a good-night kiss?

Let's take another situation. Let's suppose you've been to a movie and she invites you into her home for coffee or wine or even agrees to come to your house. You are interested in having sex with her, but you don't have a clue as to whether she'd be receptive to any touch at all from you. How do you know?

Here are some preliminary rules:

<u>Rule #1:</u> Don't assume that just because she agreed to come to your house (or invited you into hers) that it was an invitation to sex. It's not!

<u>Rule #2:</u> Accept that the woman will be making the decision about whether or not the two of you will be having sex. It's not fair, but it's the way it is.

Now that we're clear on that, let's go back to your mythical date with the woman you don't know well. You are sitting on the couch with a couple of glasses of wine in front of you. The fireplace is roaring. It's the classic romantic setting. So, does she want you to touch her? Does she want to touch you? Once again, go through the five signals. Are her eyes open? Is she sitting close to you? Is she letting her hand linger on your arm while she speaks to you? Does she lean toward you? Conversely, does she appear overly nervous or apprehensive? If you look at her, does she hold your gaze or avert it?

If her body language is giving you the go-ahead, you could reach down and take one of her hands. Hold it reassuringly, and avoid bone-crushing grabs. Above all, don't stroke her palm with your stiffened index finger. That's way too obvious.

You could also gently touch the side of her face or her neck. Try saying something like, "I'd like to touch your face. It is okay?" or "Your hair looks so (pick the appropriate word or words) cute and curly, soft and silky, shiny and sexy, or just nice. I'd like to touch it. Is that okay?" See how easy it is?

You could put an arm around her. If she stiffens up, back off. If she relaxes into your arms, good for you. If she leans down into your lap and reaches for your penis with either her hand or her mouth, even better. But that's the stuff of fantasy, and it's unlikely to happen with a woman you have just met.

Rule #3: If she says no to anything you suggest, or squirms away if you try to touch her, accept it. Pull back. Way back. Do not whine about it!! I can't tell you how much women dislike having a man whine about not getting sex. Do not say anything stupid like, "You don't know what you're missing." Do not say anything mean like, "It's okay. I wasn't that attracted to you anyway."

You can, in a friendly way, say something like, "I'm sorry. I guess I misread your signals. I thought you were attracted to me." That allows her to explain herself. She might say something like, "I am very attracted to you, but I don't want to rush forward too fast." Or "I just can't stop thinking about my niece who has measles." Or, "I want to get to know you better." It is entirely possible that she likes you a lot, but that she doesn't like being rushed.

This might be the time to move forward with some non-sexual kissing and cuddling. Here's a way of figuring out what a woman is thinking. If a woman responds to your kisses, but moves away or gets nervous when you start touching her breasts or her genitals, it often means that she likes you but she doesn't want to move as fast as you do.

Rule # 4: No groping! Ever!

Give up the idea of groping a woman. No groping, grabbing,

kneading, or squeezing! It's true that groping hasn't stopped men from being elected to public office, but that doesn't mean that women like it. Groping means grabbing or "feeling up" another person for your own sexual pleasure without that person's consent. Groping tends to feel rough, even if that's not how it's intended. Guys who grope aren't even considering what a woman might be feeling.

I'll tell you why groping is perceived as so negative. Touch, which is a very powerful form of nonverbal communication, can either relax us or make us tense. Sudden groping or grabbing activates the body's adrenaline fight or flight response. To put it bluntly, if you touch a woman in a gentle and reassuring manner, most often it will relax her. If you grope, you scare her off, and you run the risk of being left with nothing but a woman-shaped hole in your living room wall. This was Joe's problem in the beginning of the chapter.

KISSING SUGGESTIONS

Don't all romances begin with a kiss? Don't the kisses get more intense? Every woman pays a lot of attention to the first few times a man kisses her. Before you start kissing, gaze into her eyes and make sure she is responding. If she is receptive and gazes back, it's time to move on to kissing.

Put your face next to hers and nuzzle her neck. If she's wearing lipstick, smile at her and feel out how she is responding, by saying something along the order of, "I'd like to kiss you, but you're wearing lipstick. Is that okay?" Start by kissing her on the neck and side of her face. No sloppy kisses at first, please. No tongue in the ear. Lightly cup her neck, chin, or face with your hands while you kiss. Back off every once in a while and go back to gazing into her eyes. Eye gazing intensifies your connection; it helps you bond more deeply.

I personally think the first kisses should reflect the fact that you barely know each other; in other words, the mouth should be only slightly open at first. Tease each other with the promises of kisses yet to come. Let the kisses deepen as you both get more aroused. From a woman's point of view, it can be a bit intimidating when a man you barely know acts as if he is going to swallow you whole. Most women prefer the first kisses to be intense, but without excessive slobbering. After a few kisses with the mouth only slightly open, you can begin to use your tongue, but do it gently at first. Don't start exploring her dental work with your tongue until you know her better—much better.

I think the best kissers have a whole repertoire of different kinds of kisses. Some are passionate, some are intense, some are affectionate, some are loving, and some are wild. Different kisses for different moods and moments. As a sexual encounter or relationship progresses, your kisses can become more intimate and totally uninhibited. The same woman who pulls away from French kissing on the first date may well turn into a wild kisser once you have established intimacy.

The first piece of advice on kissing is to pay attention to how your partner is reacting. Is what you are doing making her move closer or is she pulling away? If you feel her stiffen or withdraw, stop what you are doing. It isn't working.

kissing do's and don'ts

- Don't glom on! What do I mean by glom on? Well, have you ever seen pictures of the remora fish stuck to the side of a shark getting a free ride? Women hate it when a man uses his mouth as though it is a magnet and she is a refrigerator.

- Don't flick your tongue in and out of your mouth like a moray eel coming out of its rock hole. Almost all women hate tongue flickers.

- Do suck gently on her bottom lip for just a few seconds.

- Do use your tongue to sensually explore the outer corners of her mouth.

- Do control your spit production. A woman doesn't want kissing to resemble using a water pik.

- Don't start licking her face and neck as though you are the family pet. If a woman really likes you, she may grow to like this approach as well, but not before the relationship becomes more intimate.

- Don't purposely inflict hickeys. It's cute when it happens on sitcoms. Less so in real life.

- Do brush your teeth before a date.

- Do think about what you eat, at least for the first few dates. Once you and your partner know each other well, you can both agree to eat garlic together.

- If you're a smoker and trying to make a really good impression on somebody you don't know well, avoid cigarettes or at least chew a couple of mints. When I asked a group of my students about this, the women felt very strongly about not wanting to kiss a man who smelled of smoke.

- Remember to keep your lips and tongue relaxed. Ditto your neck and chin. That helps you keep your kisses relaxed, soft, and sensuous.

MORE PLACES TO KISS AND TOUCH

Women love all the kissing and touching that takes place before any-body begins to remove their clothes. The other night, I was watching television with several women friends. An actor on the screen was caressing and touching a woman's face and hair. One of my friends said, " I really love it when a guy does that, don't you?" We all agreed that there is something very appealing and sexy about a man who knows how to caress and kiss a woman's hair and face. Women also love it when a man kisses their hands. I don't mean one of those for-mal top of the hand kisses reserved for nobility or the pope's ring. What I'm talking about are those spontaneous, unexpected kisses when a man takes your hand and gently kisses your palm. There is nothing wrong with kissing a woman's arm or the inside of her elbow either.

My friend Margaret has a great sexual relationship with her boyfriend, Phil. She says it got off the ground on their third date when he made her dinner and rented a video. They sat down on the couch together and he put a couch pillow on his lap and encouraged her to put her head on it and her feet up on the couch. He then caressed her hair, head, and neck while they watched the movie. She said that after thirty minutes of this, she was ready to ask him if she could spend the night. Other women have told me about men who had learned the art of foot massage (see Chapter Nine). The point of all this is that sometimes the most effective forms of touch are more sensual than sexual.

If you want to become more skillful at the art of sensual touch, the first thing you need to do is relax and enjoy the moment. Don't worry about whether or not what you are doing will lead to sex. Instead, enjoy the immediate sensations of stroking your partner's skin and hair. Gently kiss her wrist and her neck and her arms. If she is bare-legged, bend down and kiss the tops of her knees for the briefest of seconds. While she is still clothed, stroke her shoulder blades; gently touch the top of her breasts and let your fingers make a circle around her nipples. Massage her shoulders and neck and stroke her genitals through her clothing. All you have to do is relax, take it slow, and enjoy what you are doing.

TAKING OFF HER CLOTHES: SHOULD YOU?

To some degree, both men and women share the fantasy of the man skillfully and erotically removing a woman's clothing. What about the reality? I know it sounds sexy to think about undressing your partner, but have you ever tried to do it? Women's clothes are complicated. They have all kinds of hooks, buttons, and ties where you least expect them. Sometimes they come off over her head; sometimes they come down over her feet. And that's just the top layer. Who knows what else might be lurking under that cashmere sweater set with the little pearl buttons shaped like butterflies? Does this bra unhook in the front or the back? Maybe it's a sports bra and doesn't even have a hook. What about tight jeans? They look like they might be painted on, and you don't know how the heck she gets them on and off, much less expects a man to do it. Even a woman's footwear is complicated with ties, buckles, zippers, and straps. Add in the possibility of leotards, bodysuits, camisoles, and pantyhose, and you're in way over your head. So what to do?

Don't sweat it. Don't even go there. More than one sexual encounter has been stalled because of a guy trying to take off a woman's sweater with such enthusiasm that her head got stuck. It would be great if real clothes came with Velcro closures like they do in the movies so they could be ripped off without ripping, but that's not going to happen.

Many women have serious clothes issues. They don't want other people touching their clothing; they don't want big hands pawing at their delicate stuff. These women want men to notice and compliment their clothing; they don't want men to touch it. Some women have a huge psychological issue with their clothing to the point that it's a real turn-off if a man starts trying to unhook and unhinge. I'm a little bit that way myself. I'm more than willing to toss off my clothes at a moment's notice (I'm a nudist), but I don't want someone else doing it for me.

A friend of mine went on a date with a guy she was attracted to. She fully intended to have sex with him (or so she thought). That night she was wearing a nifty dress that had all kinds of little buttons down the front. I mean tiny, and there were about fifty of them. So they were sitting on the couch, kissing, and he started trying to take her dress off. Trying is the operative word because there was no way he could get those buttons undone. She said to him, "I'm not that kind of girl, but I may be by the time you get this dress off me." She went ahead and took the dress off by herself. I guess a question that could be asked (and it is one that addresses some of the complicated issues women have with clothing) is why she was wearing a dress like that in the first place.

I realize that the removal of the clothing is an important step on the way to the bed. Men say that if they start to remove a woman's shirt and she doesn't resist, it's a clear signal that she is receptive to sex. So what can you do instead? Well you can, for example, unbutton the top buttons of her shirt and kiss the tops of her breasts and see how she responds. You could slide your hand up her skirt and stroke her thighs. If she is wearing jeans and a turtle-neck, you could stroke her breasts and perhaps put your hand gently on her genitals over the jeans and see what she does. You could unbutton the top button on her jeans and gently caress her stomach or her rib cage under her breasts. The next step is a simple one: Ask. You could say something like, "If I asked you to take off your sweater, what would you say?" "How about your jeans?"

All women like to be complimented on their bodies. As your partner is removing clothing, try to say something that shows that you are paying attention to her. Try a sentence like, "You look amazing in those jeans; but even more beautiful without them."

Remember: Some of the best ways to touch a woman are by using your words and eyes to let her know that you find her exciting.

chapter four

BECOMING MORE EROTIC WITH EACH OTHER

Mark and Miranda are about to have sex for the first time, and Mark is a little bit anxious. Mark is a born salesman who likes to close his deals fast and doesn't leave his customers much room for deliberation. He's the same way about sex. Right now, he wants to have intercourse with Miranda. He wants to close the deal in the same way that he is accustomed to operating in his working world. It doesn't take a sexual genius to know that Mark's style doesn't leave much room for foreplay or erotic exploration.

Ted and Debra have been married for fifteen years. They have sex two to three times a week, and for the most part, they are both sort of satisfied with their sex life. In fact, they consider themselves lucky because they are still attracted to each other. The biggest problem with Ted and Debra's sex life is that they have a sexual routine which never varies. It's almost as though they don't have a clue about what else they could be doing sexually. I'm not talking about positions because sometimes Ted is on top, and sometimes Debra is on top. What I'm talking about is arousal and excitement and sensual exploration, not to mention conversation and communication. They are rarely really erotic with each other; they have rarely really talked about sex in a personal "when you touch me here, I feel that," kind of way. Ted, for example, is still not 100 percent sure how to give Debra an orgasm, and she's never been specific enough.

Here's a sexual misstep that most of us have taken: We move straight to intercourse without ever doing enough touching; we move straight to intercourse without doing enough talking to each other about sex, for that matter. What this means is that we never get to fully explore each other's sexuality; in the process, we often bypass being sensually erotic. This is like reaching one's destination, but missing the journey. After all, isn't getting there at least half the fun? Keep this in mind if you and your partner are just beginning a sexual relationship. If you start out on the right foot you won't have to be concerned about establishing sexual habits that are limited and limiting.

For couples who have been having sex for years, not to worry, you can still back up and take those wonderful side trips you missed; in this way you get a second chance to find out about each other's bodies and preferences. I know that couples can improve and heighten sexual intimacy, no matter how long they have known each other. For all of us, sex can be an entirely different and significantly more exciting experience.

EROTIC TOUCHING

Erotic touch is what sex is all about. Your hand touches her thigh; her hand caresses your upper arm. You come closer and feel the length of your bodies touching. Your hand touches her clitoris. Her hand strokes your scrotum. Her mouth touches your penis. Your mouth touches her breast. Your penis touches her vagina. Touch. We make love by touching one another.

When I talk about sex, I often start with information about sensate focus exercises. Sensate focus exercises were first developed by the famous sex researchers Masters and Johnson. They were originally used as a way to help couples who were having sexual difficulties. In its early days, couples using sensate focus were advised to do the following: One partner was active in that he/she was doing the pleasing and touching while the passive partner gave feedback. Many sex therapists have gone on not only to use the exercises, but to adapt them. My colleagues and I next began to advise the active partner to become more aware of what he or she was feeling, in this way removing some of the pressure from the passive partner to respond. In recent years, in my own work I've adapted these exercises further.

Don't let the name "sensate focus" mislead you. I realize it doesn't sound very sexy, but it is. This can be a totally sensual experience; I firmly believe that every single one of us can improve our sex lives by learning more about sensate focus and applying that knowledge to our own lives.

Sensate focus tells you to caress your partner's body with a light, slow, sensual touch. At this point you are probably thinking, okay, so what's new about that advice?

What's new about sensate focus is that the method asks you to concentrate all your attention on what you are feeling in your fingertips and skin. This is about the act of touching as a means of giving oneself pleasure. Yes, when you touch your partner, she will get pleasure also, but that's not where your focus should be. Your focus is on the pleasure you are receiving from what you are doing.

Couples in counseling who are given sensate focus exercises as homework are told to take turns touching each other. One partner assumes an active role while the other is passive. They are advised to stay silent and simply focus on the touch. The passive partner is encouraged to not do anything except enjoy the touch; the active partner is told to enjoy touching. Both partners are also told to concentrate on the exact point of contact where the fingers and skin make contact and to notice what feelings, positive and negative come up.

For those of you who have ever meditated, you will notice that these instructions are similar to those given for meditation: Whether you are the passive or the active partner, stay aware and in the moment and free your mind of everything but the sensation.

Touch is an essential part of lovemaking, and although we can touch each other in a myriad ways, we usually start with the hands. Women love men who know how to use their hands. Some men have an instinctive gift for touch; others are less moving. I once heard a woman named Linda say, "He thinks he's giving me pleasure, but all he's giving me is rope burn." Linda didn't want to hurt her partner's feelings, and she didn't know how to stop him and tell him what to do.

Linda is not unusual. Too often women complain to their friends about being touched the wrong way, but say nothing to their partners. The principles of sensate focus will show you how to use your hands to caress your partner.

Remember: Relaxation + Touch = Arousal.

learn her erogenous zones

Erogenous zones are those areas of the body that have a lot of nerve endings. When these places are touched, stroked, and caressed, you feel aroused and turned on. The most obvious example is the genitals. I think the head of the clitoris has something like 8,000 nerve endings; the head of the penis has about half that many. The lips and the fingertips are also rich in nerve endings. Many women say that every inch of their skin is a potential erogenous zone. Is there a woman alive who isn't turned on when a man caresses her face and neck and all the facial erogenous zones like the eyelashes, lips, and earlobes? I don't think so.

As you start to touch your partner's body, keep in mind that every part of her skin has nerve endings, as do your fingertips. Think of it all as one big erogenous zone.

CARESSING HER BREASTS

Back in my mother's day, before the sexual revolution, a guy would take a girl to the movies, put his arm around her shoulders and gradually let his hand inch down so he could touch her breasts, *over* her clothes. A couple might be dating six months to a year before the girl allowed such familiarity. It was a really big deal! This wasn't just some perfunctory stroking on the way to intercourse. Touching the breasts was the goal! The men and women I know who were dating at that time say that it was exquisitely exciting and pleasurable.

the facts about women's breasts

Until puberty, there is no real difference in breast development between boys and girls. But then, the release of estrogen and progesterone into the female body starts to create dramatic changes in the breast. Female breasts are composed of glands or lobules, milk ducts, fat, and connective tissue. The nipples themselves are rich in nerve endings which contribute to both sensitivity and pleasure. The brownish-tinged area surrounding the nipple is called the areola. The glandular tissue in the breast tends to swell and become more sensitive and tender just prior to a woman's monthly menstruation.

Just as breasts come in different shapes and sizes, there is also incredible variation in how women respond to breast stimulation. Some gauge their response level to having their nipples sucked at zero to minimal, but many more truly love having their breasts fondled, kissed, and stroked. Some women say that when their nipples are sucked, they feel as though there is a direct link going from the nipples straight down to the clitoris. They say that when their nipples are sucked, the clitoris gets hard and they begin to lubricate. There are even women who have reported that they are sometimes able to have orgasms when a man uses his hands and mouth to stimulate their breasts. Also be aware that a woman's response to breast stimulation can vary depending upon where she is in her monthly menstrual cycle.

When it comes to touching a woman's breasts, here are some suggestions:

- Be aware of how sensitive her breasts can be.
- If you nibble, do it very, very gently and only if you know she likes it.

- Don't suck too hard or bite (unless she requests it).

- Do kiss the tops of her breasts when she's wearing a low-cut top or bra. (Few women can resist this.)

- Do cup her breasts from underneath to give them support while you play with them.

- Don't squeeze, knead, pull, tug, or pinch.

- Do compliment her breasts. Something simple like "your breasts are lovely," never goes out of style. If there is something specific about them you really like, tell her. For example, "I love the way your skin feels around your nipples." Unless it's a total lie, try to emphasize the word *your*. Don't say, "God, I love breasts." Do say, "God, I love *your* breasts."

- Don't rub the palm of your hand over her nipples. This is as irritating as riding a bike while wearing a shirt that chafes your nipples.

- Don't twist her nipples as though they are radio dials.

- If you are passionate about her breasts, don't be afraid to show it. Passionate women love passion in all its forms. This is the single biggest turn-on. If her breasts give you an erection, tell her. If you fantasize about her breasts, let her know about it.

TOUCHING HER GENITALS

So let's assume that you and your sexual partner have ended up in a horizontal position, and you would like to explore her genitals. You have some choices here. If her panties are still on, should you fondle her clitoris through the fabric or reach into them through the top? Should you both get naked? Should you leave the lights on or turn them off?

As far as the lights on/lights off question, some women are shy. Personally, I prefer naked with the lights on. My second choice would be naked with a dim light or candle. But everyone is different. Some women love it when a man starts by cupping and touching her genitals while she still has her clothes on. Others love it when a man teases them by going through all the stages of clothing. First on top of the clothing, then on top of the panties, then by putting his hand into the panties to touch naked skin, and finally when she is totally naked. The first few times you are with a woman, you might opt for dim lighting. Another thing to keep in mind is the temperature of the room. If it's the dead of winter, and you are planning to bring a woman home and want to be able to lie across a bed without any clothes, remember to set your thermostat accordingly.

I know you know all this, but it has to be said. Here are two pictures of a woman's genitals. Take a look at these drawings. Think of them as maps. Before you go any further, make sure you know where everything is.

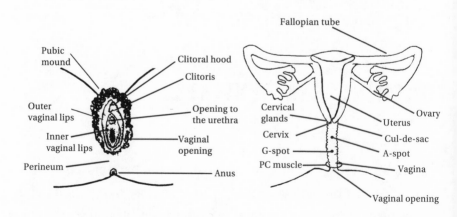

Women don't like feeling as though they are experiments for a science lab. It's important that touching her genitals is something you want to do and that you convey that to her. You can do this with words telling her that you find her beautiful and that you love the way she feels. You can do it with your eyes by gazing into hers with passion. You can do it with your lips by kissing her on her lips or on her body as you touch her genitals. You can show your excitement and passion for her genitals by the way you breathe and the expression on your face.

The following are some suggestions for how to make touching her genitals a good experience for both of you:

- Have some lubrication available. You may not need it, but you should have some choices available. There are several good choices; ask your partner if she has a preference. A water-based lubricant like K-Y Jelly or Astroglide is all-purpose, particularly if you are planning to have sex afterwards using a condom or a diaphragm. I personally like mineral oil, but because it is petroleum-based, it can and will destroy latex. That means that you shouldn't use any petroleum-based product such as Vaseline or mineral oil if you are using condoms, diaphragms, or cervical caps. Some women say that they are sensitive to petroleum products; others say that K-Y and Astroglide make them itch. Other possible choices that may be less irritating are natural oil-based products including vegetable oils, nut oils, butter, and Crisco. Be aware that these will stain your sheets, and again, don't use these with condoms, diaphragms, or cervical caps. Also don't make the mistake of using massage oils on the genitals unless the bottle specifically tells you that the ingredients are safe for internal use.

- Before you start, breathe a few times. Remind yourself not to be too rough or aggressive or you risk triggering the stress flight-or-fight response.

- Keep your touch slow and gentle. When touching her genitals, start out as slowly as you can. Keep your fingers, wrist, and hands as relaxed as possible. You can always speed up your touch or touch her more firmly as she gets more aroused or indicates that is what she wants.

- Begin your stroking and massaging on the outer edges of her body and work your way toward her clitoris and vagina. Kiss her, hold her hands. Kiss her hands; stroke her back and hips before you focus on the genitals. The bonding this establishes between you will make her more responsive. Here's another reason for doing this: It promotes blood flow toward the genitals. This will cause her clitoris and vaginal lips to fill and swell; the vagina should begin to lubricate as well.

- Don't be nervous about experimenting with different positions. Perhaps you want to start by facing each other so you can kiss while you are touching her. You could also move down between her legs so that you can look at her vagina while you're touching it.

- If you start touching her vagina, and you can feel that she's wet enough to insert your finger without forcing it, you probably won't need to use extra lubrication. But it can be fun to do so. Just ask her what she wants.

- While you are touching her genitals, she may reciprocate by reaching down to touch your penis, which is great. If she doesn't, use this time to fully explore her genitals. You don't have any pressure to use your penis or perform. Just get some quality time with her clitoris and vagina. Encourage her to just lie back and relax, and tell you what movements she likes best.

how to stimulate vaginal lubrication

The key to vaginal lubrication is found in an area inside the vagina called the anterior fornix erogenous zone. That's an intimidating name so we will call it the A spot. It's located on the front wall of the vagina between the G spot and the cervix. Researchers now believe that this area is responsible for producing most of a woman's vaginal lubrication.

When a woman likes what a man is doing and begins to feel aroused, her genitals respond accordingly. As her level of arousal increases, blood flows to the middle layer of the vagina, causing the vaginal walls to swell up. This in turn literally pushes lubrication through the inner layer of the vagina. As this begins to happen, the clitoris also swells up and becomes erect. Yes, a woman also has erectile tissue. But when a woman gets an erection, it's not just her clitoris that becomes swollen. There is a whole other mushy area of erectile tissue, known as the vaginal sponge. This area encompasses the base of the clitoris, the tissue surrounding the G spot, and the tissue surrounding the urethra and vaginal opening. If you rub a woman's A spot, you get two rewards: Her vagina will lubricate and the vaginal sponge will swell. This makes the vagina feel very tight, supple, and velvety, something you'll appreciate even more when you start having actual intercourse.

To stimulate a woman's A spot, gently insert a finger (lubricated of course) into her vagina as far as it will comfortably go. Keep your fingers and hand relaxed and rub ever so gently between the G spot and the cervix. Use the whole length of your finger. Still confused about where the A spot is? Remember that the A spot is on the front wall of the vagina. When you touch the front wall, you are touching her abdomen, but from the inside. Do this for a few minutes and see how much lubrication it creates. Some women, of course, lubricate very little. With others, you might have to hang on to the side of the mattress so you don't get washed overboard like George Clooney in *The Perfect Storm*.

ASKING HER WHAT SHE WANTS

Learning to talk to your partner about her sexual preferences is part and parcel of being a good and confident lover. Most women like to talk about what they want, but find it hard to initiate these conversations. They are typically happy when a man is confident enough to encourage them to do so.

If you were lucky enough to be sitting in the center of a room surrounded by women who were masturbating, you would discover that there are a wide variety of different ways for a woman to touch herself. Some women use one hand; some use two; some women stimulate the clitoris with one hand while they use the other to apply pressure to the opening of the vagina; some prefer to masturbate with a dildo or a vibrator. Some women like to masturbate in the tub, using water from the shower or faucet to provide additional stimulation on the clitoris. When you touch a woman's genitals as I suggested, I can guarantee that she will be aroused and stimulated. However, there may still be something more or different that she would like you to do. Asking a woman about her sexual needs can be a bit tricky. Here are some suggestions:

- Try to convey your passion and your enthusiasm for your partner. Say something like, "I really want to get to know everything about you. Let me know how you want me to touch you."

- Ask her to show you as in, "Take my hand and put it exactly where you want it to be. Move my hand exactly the way you want me to move it." Ask her, "Do you want me to put my finger here? Or here? Where is it best?" Ask her to tell you, "Do you want it slower? Faster?"

- Be very careful not to express any judgments or disdain for what she says. Don't get a sarcastic tone, whatever she tells you. Don't say anything like, "You want me to do what? Are you crazy?" If you are really turned off by something she suggests, offer an alternative suggestion.

- Get comfortable talking about sex. Don't be embarrassed. And whatever you do, don't start making jokes to hide your feelings.

- Find words that you are both comfortable about using. It helps if you and your partner can find ways of describing body parts, and it helps if you can find ways to describe what you are doing. There are so many names that we use for our genitals. Both you and your partner might be happy retaining the technical penis, clitoris, and vagina, but you might also want to experiment. If you're going to use slang terms and nicknames, keep in mind that most women don't like ones that sound degrading and prefer those that convey affection.

TELLING HER WHAT YOU WANT

Most women find it a total turn-on when a man shows her how to touch his body, particularly if it is done in an intimate way. Try to keep what you are doing and saying personal. You can, for example, gaze into her eyes. Then take her hand, while holding her gaze, and say, "Let me show you how I like it best." Hold the eye contact as much as possible. This is about developing communication between you and your partner. By the way, don't ever say anything like, "This is how Debbie did it," or "Let me show you how Mary used to suck my balls."

Women don't like it if they feel that men are simply "using" their partners' bodies without any intimacy. They like sex to be an intimate and erotic experience between two people. What that means is that they hate it when a man gets overly instructional, as in, "Touch here. Touch there," without conveying a feeling of connection. Some sentences that you can use are, "I'd love to have *you* touch me . . . here." "I love the way your hands feel on my body, could you put them on my . . ." "You have such a sensual mouth . . . I'd love to feel it on my . . ."

Don't be afraid to express what you like and show your partner what you want. In the context of a close relationship, helping a partner explore your sensuality is a good thing.

DON'T FORGET YOUR MOUTH AND TONGUE

We've put so much focus on what to do with your hands that I don't want you to forget that you also have a mouth. Use it. Mouth-to-skin contact is an erotic and sensual experience for both partners. Don't limit your mouth to kissing. Use your tongue to explore parts of her body that you might never have thought of as sensual. Kiss the inside of her elbow and then use your tongue to draw a line down to her wrist. Kiss her shoulder and use your tongue to guide you to a nipple. Treat her like she's a piece of delicious fruit that you want to suck and draw into your mouth. Trust me, she'll like it.

HELPING YOUR PARTNER RELAX

Marissa and Frank have been together about a year. They are very attracted to each other, and sex is always great. They see each other mostly on weekends because Marissa, a single mother, often has baby-sitting issues during the week. It's Saturday night and Frank has been looking forward to seeing Marissa all week. She is coming to his house for dinner, and he expects that it will be a romantic sexy evening.

Marissa's son is spending the weekend with his father, and Frank is positive that as soon as Marissa walks through the door of his apartment, they will both be ready to fling off their clothes and hop into bed. He sure is! But surprise! When Marissa walks through the door, she is annoyed and short-tempered. Her ex-husband was late; her son was cranky; and as Marissa was leaving her house, her mother had phoned with a series of strange demands. Marissa looks as though she is more in the mood for kick-boxing than sex. But despite the way she looks, Frank is still not sure. It's possible that some physical contact would help Marissa relax.

Both men and women need to be at least a little bit relaxed in order to be receptive to touch. It's difficult to get aroused when you're totally stressed. You know how a car with a manual transmission has to go through neutral to get to the higher gears? Well, your body has to do the same thing.

One of the things a man sometimes has to do is learn to assess his partner's mood to know whether she is receptive to touch. In the last chapter, I talked about how to use nonverbal communication in a situation with a new partner. It's equally important that you use it in situations with your long-term girlfriend or wife. You need to let her nonverbal communication tell you what her current mood state is and whether she's receptive to having sex.

Let's say you really don't have a clue as to her mood because she's not telling you, and she's not really putting out anything in the way of nonverbal messages, positive or negative. Throw out a line and do a little fishing. Let's say the feeling between you is generally positive, or at least neutral and not negative. Use eye gaze and touch to try to intensify the positive feelings in the situation. Put an arm around her and look into her eyes. If she gazes back, I see nothing wrong with moving ahead. If she detaches or pulls away, don't push it. Back off. She's not in a sexual mood yet. Better to start by suggesting something that is relaxing.

Suppose your partner comes home from work and she's visibly stressed out and upset. Because you're a nice guy, your first impulse might be to give her a hug. With some women, this is a terrific thing to do. With others, however, touch might intensify the negativity of the situation. Most women appreciate it when you give them a chance to take off their shoes and relax a little. If your partner is tense, put your sexual agenda on hold; pour her a glass of wine, listen to what's upsetting her, and allow her time to unwind.

Try to breathe in a calm, even way. Pace your voice to help her relax. Emotions are contagious, and we all influence each other's emotional state. But if one person is in an up mood while the other is in a down mood, one person's emotional state may take over. What will determine whose mood ends up controlling the emotional energy between you? Some people seem to have a greater chance of influencing someone else's mood while others are just naturally more suggestible or easily influenced. In the end though, the main factor is intention. If you are motivated to change your partner's mood, there is a good chance you will be able to do so. So if your partner is in a crummy mood, your challenge is to lift her up as opposed to getting pulled down.

There is a wide variety of things that a man can do to help a woman relax and transition to a better space. Think about things that will bring you closer and help you communicate. How about any of the following: taking a walk together; taking a nap together; or taking a bath together.

MASTURBATION WITH A PARTNER

Touching ourselves sexually is a totally intimate experience. Sharing it with a partner will, almost by definition, deepen and intensify our sense of connection and trust.

There are several ways to approach this experience. You could say, "I think we would be closer if we could masturbate together." Or "I want to know how you give yourself sexual pleasure so I could learn." Or "I want you to see how I touch myself so that you can know more about me."

Some couples like to start out masturbating next to each other and making eye contact while they do so. Another way is for each partner to masturbate alone while the other watches. Sometimes the watcher can join in by cuddling, holding, kissing, or caressing the partner who is masturbating. Sometimes when two people are masturbating and making contact as they do so, they get so turned on, that they end up having intercourse anyway, which is fine. It is a good idea, though, to learn more about your partner's masturbatory style. It will help your lovemaking.

Cuddling, caressing, and kissing a partner who is masturbating are ways of expressing unconditional acceptance. Masturbating together can also show total acceptance. Masturbating in front of someone is a very trusting thing to do. When you do this, I think it's helpful to discuss some of your feelings about masturbating together. You don't want it to become "your little secret" that never gets talked about because that defeats the concept of intimacy.

Mutual masturbation can be very helpful on those nights when you are both too tired and stressed to have sex, but still would benefit from sexual release. Remember that mutual masturbation is not about retreating from your partner into your own universe; it's about sharing and becoming closer.

chapter five

DON'T BE SHY ABOUT ORAL SEX

One morning as I was on my way to teach my class, I realized I was early and needed to kill some time. So I stopped at a bookstore. Whenever I go into a bookstore, I head straight for the sexuality section. I always want to see if anyone has written anything new; for me, this is research. I've spent enough time in bookstores to know that, even in the neatest establishment, the shelves that store the books on sex are always messed up. I think what happens is that people pick up books and start reading them, then look around to see if anyone sees them reading sex books and get embarrassed. That's when they throw the books back in any old place on the bookshelves. If you're looking for a specific book on sexuality, you have to search through the entire section because everything is always out of order.

On this particular day, there were only a couple of other customers in the store. I started browsing through the sex section and this guy wandered over near me. He was a little bit on the nerdy side. I noticed that he was staring at me as I looked at the books, and I could tell he wanted to say something. I sort of ignored him, but finally he said, "Can I ask you a question?" I was about to say "no," but for some reason I changed my mind and said, "Okay." Keep in mind that this guy had no idea who I am or that I teach sexuality. For all he knew, I was just some horny broad in the sex section of the bookstore.

He cleared his throat and asked me a question. "Do women like oral sex?" At this point, I probably should have called the manager and said that there was some pervert harassing me, but for some reason, instead, I answered him, "Do you mean, do they like giving it or getting it?"

He said, "Getting it."

I made the decision to try to answer him honestly, "Some women do, and some women don't. I'm assuming that you're only planning on having oral sex with one woman at a time, so you only need to know whether that particular woman likes oral sex. However, the odds are in your favor because a lot of women like oral sex." Then I recommended a couple of books that had oral sex techniques and I pulled them off the shelf and handed them to him.

Of course, when I left the bookstore, I was thinking, "Why did he ask me *that* question?" and "Why did he ask *me* that question?" In answer to *your* question, yes, I do think he was trying to hit on me, and how pathetic is that? What did he expect me to do, lie down, spread my legs, and holler, "Bring it on!"? I'm sure he got a more detailed answer than he bargained for. Thinking about it right now, I realize I probably should have charged him for the sexual advice.

However, as creepy as this guy's approach was, I think his question reflected some genuine confusion that other men share. Yes, there are many, many women who enjoy receiving oral sex quite a lot. But there are some who don't.

Why don't all women like oral sex? Well, there are women who don't like it because they have somehow been convinced that their vagina smells, tastes, or looks unappealing. They have been influenced by people who think the female genitals are ugly—and that's a shame. Some women say that they just don't feel that much from oral sex. They sometimes say that when they receive oral sex, it's a ticklish and negative feeling. There are also some women who are embarrassed about oral sex because they get *too* much enjoyment from it. My advice to you is that there is only one woman you need to worry about, and that's the one you are with right now.

The same is true about giving oral sex. Some women love to do it so much that it almost doesn't matter who the guy is. These women say it's a tremendous turn-on; they are aroused by watching and experiencing a man's reactions; they love feeling his excitement. Frequently, women say that it gives them a sense of power and an understanding of what men must feel when they make love to a woman.

On the other side of the coin, there are women who won't give oral sex under any circumstances, even with somebody they totally adore. A woman with this attitude may say that she just doesn't like the idea of putting her mouth on a man's penis. She may say that she is afraid she is going to gag, or that she is afraid of the taste of semen. Some women say that oral sex reminds them of man-on-man sex in a negative way.

Of course, there are also a great many women who enjoy oral sex up to the point where a man starts to ejaculate, and then they just want to remove their mouths as soon as possible, often quickly substituting a hand. Some women don't mind the taste of semen, but don't want to swallow; these women are perfectly content so long as they can spit it out or let it dribble out of their mouth. Still others love everything about giving oral sex and swallow without thinking about it twice.

Years ago, there was a great deal of stigma attached to oral sex. In fact, oral sex between consenting adults was illegal in some states, as were many other non-reproductive sexual practices such as same-sex sex and anal sex. Much of that was changed by the sexual revolution of the 1960s and 1970s. Not only is oral sex now legal, it's hugely popular. We have a number of things to thank for that, including an ex-president who inadvertently gave news commentators a chance to repeat the phrase "oral sex" over and over again on the nightly news until it became a commonplace household expression.

These days, oral sex is so far out of the closet that you can even find oral sex trainers who will come to your house and demonstrate how to give blow jobs using soup spoons and dildos, as well as various fruits and vegetables. Some of these training classes are even taught to straight women by gay men. There are also classes available for men who want to learn more about how to satisfy a woman with oral sex. Some of these have made it on to cable television. The one I happened to catch one night when I was up very late encouraged men to use luscious fruits like mangoes for practice.

BECOMING A VAGINA MAN

Do you think of yourself as a leg man, a breast man, or an ass man? Is there another part of the female anatomy you find particularly appealing? Here's a fact: If you want to be good at doing oral sex on a woman, you're going to have to become a vagina man and/or a clit man. In order to become really good at oral sex, you have to learn to worship at the entrance of the sacred feminine city.

what lesbians can teach you about oral sex

Oral sex is the most common sexual practice in woman/woman relationships. It's almost impossible to be a lesbian without enjoying oral sex. Surveys show that lesbians report more orgasms with woman-on-woman oral sex than straight women do with man-on-woman oral sex. So what is their secret?

Lesbians love the vagina, and they love the clitoris. To get some lesbian oral sex techniques, rent a woman-on-woman–oriented sex video or DVD. Don't make the mistake of renting the kind of video that shows two women doing each other for the enjoyment of a male third party. Rent the kind that's intended for lesbian audiences.

o with their tongues.

ıe

get as much pleasure as you can from giving oral pleasure to your partner, you need to become more aware of your tongue. The tongue is full of nerve endings which can give you, as well as your partner, a wide variety of sensual experiences. To get a sense of how many, the next time you are at the market, buy yourself a really juicy piece of fruit, like a mango, for example. When you get it home, cut yourself a triangular piece of it. Pretend for a few minutes that this piece of fruit represents your partner's genitals. Lick it and suck on it. Allow your tongue to explore the surface of the fruit. Use each side of your tongue and slowly slide the side along the fruit. Keep the tip of your tongue soft and lap at the fruit; stiffen the tip of your tongue a little bit and move it back and forth. See what I mean about sensitivity?

The same techniques you use to eat certain foods will apply to oral sex. Think about how you eat an ice cream cone by swirling your tongue around the edges. One of my students said that she wished her boyfriend would go down on her like he was lapping melted chocolate from a wrapper. I personally think a man should perform oral sex as if he was eating a peach or an orange or even a watermelon. There's a certain amount of joyous slurping involved.

I like to encourage people who want to perform oral sex to get their tongue muscles into better shape. Remember the importance of your PC muscle to your sexuality? The muscles in your tongue are just as important. Here are some simple exercises to improve your skills at oral lovemaking. I know that these exercises sound kind of goofy and look weird, but they really work.

The Tongue Push Up

Stand in front of a mirror and curl your tongue up so that the tip of the underside of the front half is up against the roof of your mouth. Repeat. When you look at your open mouth in the mirror, you will see the underside of your tongue. This can be surprisingly difficult to do at first, but it is one of the best tongue exercises I know.

Tongue Curls

Curl the side edges of your tongue up and then let your tongue go flat. Repeat.

I read somewhere that the ability to do this exercise is genetic so some of you will have a harder time than others. It's okay to push your tongue out of your mouth to do this.

Tongue Stretches

Stick your tongue straight out of your mouth as far as it will go.

Then move it back into your mouth. Repeat.

Stick your tongue out of your mouth and try to touch your nose. Now try to touch your chin. Repeat.

Repeat these exercises 10–20 times. Try to do them three times a week.

Trust me. After you've done tongue exercises for a while, your partner won't be able to watch you eat an ice cream cone without getting turned on. An additional benefit of these exercises is that they supposedly fight wrinkles and sagging and help keep your face looking young.

HOW TO GO DOWN ON HER

It's probably easiest for a woman to have an orgasm when she is lying on her back so encourage her to do that. If you want her to be even more comfortable, put a pillow under her butt. Tell her to close her eyes and relax. Some women like to keep their legs fully extended, but others may bend one or both of them.

Relaxation and surrender are the key ingredients of good oral sex. This is true for both partners. Before you start, take a couple of calming breaths and remind yourself not to tense up; keep your chin, neck, tongue, and lips relaxed. Position yourself directly in front of her genitals. You don't want to end up with a stiff neck so place your body in a way that is comfortable for you.

With oral sex, remember to start slowly and gently. Don't let your lips or tongue dry out because the absence of lubrication can be irritating to a woman's genitals. Similarly if you have a rough new growth of beard, you might want to shave before you begin oral sex.

Start by kissing her inner thighs and using your tongue to explore. Don't be afraid to lap with your tongue. Think of a cat lapping up cream from a saucer, and enjoy the sensations your tongue is experiencing.

For the vast majority of women, the clitoris is the most likely source of orgasm. It's like Old Faithful. Lick up both sides of the clitoris. Gently suck on it. When you're starting out, be tender and exploratory. Don't press your face into her clitoris until she is really aroused. Remember that as far as the clitoris is concerned, different women have different levels of sensitivity. Some, for example, like it when a man immediately moves the clitoral hood away and focuses directly on the clitoris itself. Others say that they hate that sensation until they are fully aroused; still others have told me that they are so sensitive that they never want the hood to be pulled away because they find this level of direct stimulation more painful than exciting, no matter what their level of arousal. It's up to you to ask your partner how sensitive she is and what she likes best. Also, remember that some women are more sensitive on one side of the clitoris or vagina than the other. Ask your partner if this is true for her.

Tease her PC muscle by flicking your tongue an inch in and out of her vagina. Gently insert a relaxed finger into her vagina and softly rub her G spot or A spot. Gently push up on her clitoris and lick underneath it. This is the U Spot or urethral area. Some women find it exciting to have this spot gently licked, but don't get rough because the area is delicate and easily irritated.

Whenever you do oral sex, try to do what feels good to you. The most important thing to remember is to show your enthusiasm. It's important for a woman to feel that her partner enjoys doing oral sex. She wants her partner to like her genitals. If you act as though you are performing a chore, she isn't going to be able to relax.

Many women tense their legs as they get more aroused and closer to orgasm. Keep an eye on her responses. Is she getting more excited? If she is, it's important for a man to remember that whatever he is doing, it's working. Put your hand on her breast. Is her heart beginning to beat faster; is her breathing telling you anything? Some men, when they realize a woman is about to orgasm, make the mistake of changing what they are doing. They may be trying to increase her pleasure, but instead they may simply bring it to a halt. In short, if a specific motion of the tongue or mouth seems to be bringing your partner to orgasm, keep doing just that.

other positions for oral sex

Here are some variations that might appeal to you and your partner.

The Seated Woman

Some couples like to do oral sex with the woman seated on a sofa or a chair and the man on his knees in front of her. In a variation on this, the woman can be seated on a kitchen table or island with the man facing her on a stool or chair. Men may find this position puts less strain on their necks.

Woman on Top

Some men like to do oral sex while reclining comfortably on their backs. The woman straddles the man's shoulders, facing in either direction, while resting her weight on her knees.

Side by Side

There are always some comfort advantages to having both partners

lie on their sides. You can rest your head on her thigh or on a small pillow leaning against her thigh, for example. The only problem is that
many women find it harder to reach an orgasm in this position.

You Do Me and I'll Do You

At one time, the concept of the so-called 69 position was considered totally titillating and erotic. And, in fact, many men still fantasize about it. In reality, however, this position can have some serious
drawbacks. Many men and women complain that it is distracting
and difficult to focus on either the giving or the receiving. Some of
the pleasure of being the receiver of oral sex comes with the sense of
not having anything to do except letting go and abandoning yourself to the sensation. This element is lost when you are also actively
trying to bring your partner to orgasm; it's also true that some of the
satisfaction that accompanies being the one to pleasure your partner is gone because you tend to lose concentration.

if you get tired

I once heard a man complaining about giving oral sex to a woman
who had a difficult time reaching orgasm. He said that she told him
that the only way she could reach orgasm was if he repeatedly
flicked his tongue over one specific spot on her clitoris while he
simultaneously twirled her left nipple with his right hand. He swore
that he did that for a full twenty minutes to no avail. By then, his
neck was so stiff that he got up and got an ice pack out of the freez-
er. He says he used his left hand to hold the ice pack on his neck and
he went back to licking and twirling for twenty more minutes. Now,
I have to tell you right now that this guy was the kind of person who
couldn't resist a good story, so this anecdote may have been totally

apocryphal. Nonetheless, I want you to understand that sometimes women can't reach orgasms. If you and your partner are having oral sex, and you are exhausted, and it has become apparent that nothing is working, it's okay to stop. Just switch to intercourse or some cuddling to transition. I want to remind you, however, that even if your partner can't quite manage an orgasm, she may still be feeling very turned on and vulnerable to you. What this means is that at these moments, it's probably not totally sensitive to immediately turn on the ball game and grab a beer. You may want to transition to intercourse, or if you have already had an orgasm and can't immediately manage another erection, spend some time cuddling.

SHAVING FOR WOMEN

I'm a big believer in shaving, and I would encourage all women to get on the bandwagon and see for themselves how shaved pubic hair can increase sexual pleasure. I firmly believe that there is no comparison between receiving oral sex with pubic hair and without. With shaved pubic hair, the clitoris is so much more exposed and sensitive that it sometimes makes the difference between a woman who is orgasmic and one who is not.

Women can shave their pubic hair using either a regular blade razor, a disposable razor, an electric razor designed for women, or a man's beard trimmer. More and more women are beginning to opt for hair removal with waxing, electrolysis, or laser.

This discussion reminds me of the joke about the busy and frazzled woman who goes to the beauty parlor and says to the hairdresser, "I swear! I'm so stressed I don't know which end is up," and the hairdresser says, "Well, honey, you better decide, 'cause

I'm fixin' to start shampooing."

The first time a woman shaves her pubic hair, she will probably want to start by trimming some of the thicker clumps using scissors. For the shaving itself, she can either shave wet using soap or gel, or shave dry using baby powder. Somebody showed me how to do this, and although I was a little skeptical, it worked really well. Just put baby powder on the pubic mound and then dry shave it with a *new* disposable razor. This gives a really close shave. It obviously doesn't work on the vaginal lips. I find that a beard trimmer (they cost about thirty dollars) is best for that.

A combination that I've found works well is to shave the pubic mound, outer lips, and inner thighs every day in the shower with soap or gel. Every third day or so, you can use the beard trimmer to get rid of stubble on the inner and outer lips, as well as the area around the clitoris. When it comes to using the beard trimmer, stand with one leg up on the bathroom sink and gently spread your vaginal lips first to one side and then the other. It takes a little practice. At first, it's kind of like trying to shave a piece of sushi.

For men, if you want to volunteer to shave your girlfriend, just be super careful of nicks. Go very slow and gentle. Remember not to put a beard trimmer into a thick clump of hair because it can get caught. Make sure you have good lighting and can see what you're doing. Have your partner show you how much pressure to use.

FOOD AND ORAL SEX

I've always thought that watching some people eat is very sexy. I used to have a boyfriend who was the sexiest eater. He didn't do it on purpose; it was just his style of eating. He savored every bite so that you knew he paid attention to sex.

People who pay attention to their food pay attention to oral sex. If you want women to find you attractive, learn to be a sexy eater. This is nothing as obvious as licking your tongue over your lips or sticking it in and out of your mouth and leering. That's gross! Also gross is watching someone who eats like a pig or shovels their food in and doesn't really pay attention to how it tastes. A man who is a sexy eater eats slowly, appreciates food that tastes great in his mouth, has great table manners, and pays attention to every bite.

Having said that, you're probably expecting me to give you instructions about how to put food on you and your partner's genitals and eat it off. Surprise! That's not going to happen. While it is generally safe to put food like whipped cream on the penis, you really shouldn't put any foods into the vagina because it can disturb the delicate Ph (acid/alkaline) balance of the vagina and cause a vaginal infection. Another thing not to do is drink champagne and do oral sex with your partner while the champagne is in your mouth. Alcohol burns. Personally, I don't get the attraction of putting food on the genitals and eating it off. To me, it sounds as appetizing as eating an ice cream cone and finding pubic hairs in it. I think some of the whipped cream advocates may still be a little bit uncomfortable with oral sex and are trying to find a way to disguise what they are doing. If you want to add flavor to the oral experience, I think you're better off using a flavored lotion or gel from an adult store. They come in a zillion flavors and textures and are designed to be used on the genitals. However, even with these, some women are super-sensitive.

BECOMING THE KIND OF GUY WHOSE PENIS WOMEN WANT TO SUCK

Oral sex is something men like as much as women. However, many women are hesitant about oral sex because they've had bad experiences with it. What constitutes a bad experience? Here are a couple of examples of situations that most women don't like.

Manny has encouraged Suzie to perform oral sex. He's having such a good time that he's put off his orgasm, and now his orgasm appears to have retreated and is moving further and further away. Manny, however, is determined to climax, no matter how long it takes Suzie to make it happen. Suzie has been working on it for more than twenty minutes. It has become an unpleasant chore. Her neck hurts, her mouth hurts, and her knees hurt. She is acutely uncomfortable. To compound her discomfort, Manny keeps giving her instructions of the "go harder," "faster," "grab my balls" variety. As much as Suzie likes sex, what is even more important to her right now is that she is bored out of her mind. She wonders, "Would Manny mind if I turned on the TV?" She also wonders, "Will this ever end?"

Vincent's girlfriend Justine is sexually inexperienced and reluctant to do certain things in bed. Performing oral sex is one of them. Nonetheless, Vincent convinces her that she will enjoy it. She wants to please him so she agrees to give it a try. Following Vincent's instructions, she takes his penis in her mouth. Her first thought is, "This isn't too terrible. I could learn to like this." Within minutes, however, Vincent's arousal level goes through the roof. He grabs Justine by the head and pushes her mouth down while he vigorously thrusts his penis into her mouth. A couple of shudders and spasms later, he has ejaculated deep into her throat. Justine's gag reflex becomes fully operative, and she runs into the bathroom shuddering and shaking, vowing, "Never again!"

I share these stories with you so that you will realize that many women are hesitant to perform oral sex because they have had bad experiences. In fact, like Justine, some women have one bad first experience and never want to do it again. They become gun-shy and think things like, "Don't point that thing at me; it might go off."

making oral sex more appealing to her

Here are some thoughts to help make you the lucky recipient of frequent blow jobs:

- Discuss some of the issues of oral sex *before* anyone starts doing anything. You could say something like, "Hey, I want you to be comfortable with this so I'm going to tell you before I start to have an orgasm. That way, I won't take you by surprise." You may be with a woman who wants to get her mouth out of the way before you come; you may be with a woman who prefers to spit out the semen; or you may be with a woman who wants to swallow. You will find out soon enough. After you've had sex with this woman a few times, this is something you can discuss in greater depth.

- Make sure your penis and the entire genital area have been recently washed. The whole package should look appetizing and clean.

- Many women really appreciate an attractive shave job with smooth testicles and no stray hairs. Loose pubic hairs can really cause you to gag.

- Don't use deodorant-type products or powders in the area because they taste terrible.

- Don't pull her hair or grab her ears.

- Don't ask her to involve herself in any peculiar contortions so that you can grab or pinch body parts.

- Don't push her head in a rough way. That means not pushing it down or up and down.

- Don't do anything that makes her feel confined or pinned down by your genitals in any way. She should always be able to remove her mouth quickly if she chooses.

- Encourage her to hold on to the base of your penis to keep it from going in too far and stimulating her gag reflex. If she doesn't immediately understand the concept, hold it yourself.

- Give her some feedback about your arousal levels on the 1–10 scale described in Chapter Two so she can gauge how close you are to coming.

- Try to keep your penis still so as not to cause her to feel overpowered. If you feel that you must thrust, keep your movement gentle.

- Remember that this is something that she is doing, so try not to give her too many instructions. Tell her what you like, but give her the chance to find her own creativity about where and how to kiss, suck, or lick.

- Be predictable. This is very important! She's most likely to enjoy doing oral sex if she knows your arousal pattern.

- Allow yourself to ejaculate quickly and easily if you can. If you know you have a tough time ejaculating during oral sex, don't make your partner work so hard that her neck and shoulders ache. Use oral sex as foreplay and move on to intercourse while she is still enthusiastic.

- Encourage your partner to start doing oral sex on you before you have an erection. Many women say it's a turn-on to feel a man get hard in their mouths.

- Pique her curiosity. Women are interested in what happens when you ejaculate. They like to feel your PC muscle spasm.

- Have tissues or a towel handy so one of you can wipe up the semen.

- When you reach the point of inevitability, tell her you're going to come so she can make her own decision about where or where not to put her mouth.

- Be enthusiastic about what she is doing. Articulate your pleasure. Tell her which movements really work.

- After it's over, show her that you appreciate her effort. Tell her what really excited you and what you enjoyed most.

- Be loving and affectionate.

- Very important: Don't recoil from kissing her because she has just had semen in her mouth.

TELLING WOMEN WHAT YOU LIKE

One of the ways a man becomes a better lover is by letting his partner know what he likes. This is particularly true of oral sex. Men, let your partner know that you find oral sex exciting in general, and that the idea of her mouth going down on you is even more exciting. Remember that your partner's attitude toward sex is always going to be more personal and less generalized than yours. She wants to know that you want *her* mouth on your penis, not just *a* mouth on your penis.

Tell her that you like it when she starts slowly. Tell her that you like it when she licks your balls. Suggest that she gently suck on your testicles, one at a time and ask her to lick the area right behind the testicles. Show her how she can hold (not grab) your penis at the base with one hand. Tell her to slowly suck the head in and out of her mouth, and then move down the shaft, sucking a quarter- or a half-inch more each time. When you feel your arousal rising, gently suggest that she start speeding up the motion. Tell her how you want her to alternate sucking and licking around the sides of the penis, like an ice cream cone. Tell her to hold your balls as your arousal increases so that she can feel the first PC muscle spasm that will signal that you are about to come. If you want her to lightly squeeze your balls, make sure you let her know.

There are several popular positions for oral sex on a man. A woman can kneel next to him or between his legs. The man can sit on a chair, and the woman can kneel between his legs. The man leans against a wall with the woman on her knees or on a chair in front of him. Another favorite of many men is for the woman to lie on her side with her male partner kneeling upright next to her. In this way she can lick the underside of his penis and suck on it from underneath. The man's view of this is incredible, sort of like having his own porno movie.

chapter six

LET'S TALK ABOUT THE "I" WORD

What do you mean when you tell a friend that you "had sex?" Like most of us, you are probably referring specifically to the act of intercourse. Have you noticed how few people ever use the "I" word? People seem to prefer a wide variety of other terms and words. Some of them are just plain childish; others, of course, we can't print in this book. I remember back in high school when people used to call it "going all the way."

Do you remember the events surrounding the first time you had intercourse? Of course you do. That's because intercourse is such a big deal. Think about it. For most people, intercourse is the centerpiece of every intimate romantic relationship; intercourse is how two people make babies; intercourse is the most intimate thing that two people can do together. Is anything else we do more fun, more thrilling, more satisfying, and more potentially life-altering than sexual intercourse? Doesn't it make sense that we should all spend a little bit of time learning how to be better (and wiser) at doing something "that comes naturally?"

THRUSTING AND THE MALE ROLE DURING INTERCOURSE

No matter what position the couple decides to use for intercourse, the man still tends to be the dominant partner. By the time he's finished this book, I hope my male reader will be able to have intercourse for as short or long a time period as he wants. Nonetheless, the length of time a man maintains an erection pretty much determines whether the couple will be having intercourse for five minutes or thirty minutes. The pacing of each sexual session also tends to be dependent on the man. Is he, for example, stroking fast or slow, and does he have rhythm?

Many men don't spend enough time thinking about what I would call male rhythm; instead, they establish a pattern and stay with it. However, a man can train himself to alter the rhythm with which he thrusts during intercourse. Most experienced women will tell you that a great lover is like a great deejay in that he knows how to mix and match his rhythms. Sometimes he thrusts with a deliciously slow and sensual tempo; other times he has the pace of a great drummer during a prolonged roll.

When I'm working with a man who wants to improve his lovemaking skills, I often suggest that he begin listening to music and moving his body as he would when he is thrusting during intercourse. I used to play the piano, and one of the ways that helped me get more control as a musician was to try to play the same piece at different speeds. When I practiced a slow piece, sometimes I would do it very fast. In this way, when I slowed it down to the right tempo, I would have more control. When I practiced a fast piece at a slow tempo, it would also give me more control. I used to think about my early piano lessons when I talked to men about exactly how to thrust.

If you want your partner to say, "Wow, he's got rhythm!" here is my best advice: Practice thrusting with different pieces of music. Go with the rhythm and practice, practice, practice. Practice your thrusting with hip-hop, country, and oldies but goodies. Don't forget folk or any other kind of music. All music has rhythm; that's why it's music. As far as intercourse is concerned, you want to be able to move to the music, even when it's not playing.

RHUMBA ANYONE?

Tom and Suzanne are new lovers. They like each other a lot, and Tom is thinking that Suzanne could be "the one." However, he has always had a major concern about marriage: He worries about the sex becoming boring. He doesn't ever want his sex life to become routine. With that in mind, he wants the two of them to have sex in every conceivable position in every room in the house. He wants to experiment and try new things. He has never, for example, had sex on a kitchen table. He's seen it done in movies and thinks it's something he should experience at least once. Tom lives in a studio apartment with a galley kitchen, but Suzanne has a sturdy-looking table in her dining area, and he would love to try having sex on it. He'd also like to try stuff that is just a little more adventurous. Tom's friend Peter is having a party next week, and he wonders if Suzanne would be willing to have sex in Peter's bathroom while the party is in full swing. Just thinking about it makes Tom excited.

There are so many different ways to have sex. "So many ways, so little time," as a friend of mine is fond of saying. Intercourse involves two people moving together and trying to find each other's rhythm. Think of it like dancing. When people decide to go out dancing together, they have choices. They could do the tango, foxtrot, polka, or Texas two-step. With sex, we also have the choice of several different positions, each with its own pros and cons.

I think before we start talking about various positions, we have to understand that there are no rules that say one position is better than any other. There are also no rules telling you that you can't keep using the same old position every time you have sex. If it's working for both partners, why not, if that's what you want to do.

Nonetheless, I think it's smart to think about and be aware of some of the different intercourse positions and variations. If nothing else, it will help you understand why you prefer the positions you do. Sometimes we cling to certain positions for reasons that have nothing to do with pleasure. Women particularly may avoid some sexual positions because they worry that they don't look like movie or television stars; sometimes they may need coaxing to help them get past old inhibitions. A man who is able to show his partner that he accepts and likes her body can usually convince her to become more experimental. I think most women are usually happy when a man encourages them to let go of some of their insecurities. This is about being a sensitive lover, and it doesn't always happen overnight.

Here are some of the most common sexual positions and their pros and cons.

male superior position

In the basic missionary position, the woman lies flat on her back while the man lies on top of her. There are, of course, several variations. The man can support himself on his elbows and knees or on his palms and feet. There is also a variation known as the CAT or coital alignment technique. In this position, the man pulls himself up and forward toward the woman's shoulders so that his pubic bone is rubbing against her clitoris, and his penis is going into her more vertically than horizontally. This position can be varied a good deal depending on the positioning of the legs. A woman can leave her legs flat, bend her knees, raise her legs into the air, or wrap them around her partner's body.

Pros

- For a man, this is usually one of the most arousing positions.
- It contributes to a feeling of bonding and intimacy because the couple can easily make eye contact, talk, and kiss.
- This is the most culturally sanctioned position.
- Many people find it a turn-on when the man is the more dominant and aggressive partner.

Cons

- It is one of the least effective positions for clitoral stimulation.
- Some men find it harder to delay ejaculation in this position.
- Some men say that supporting their weight in this position can be tiring.
- This position doesn't give the depth of penetration of some of the others.

female superior position

This is the classic woman on top position. The man lies flat on his back while his partner is on top, facing him. Her legs can be placed in several ways. One woman might enjoy lying on top in such a way that there is total body contact, her legs resting on his. Another woman might prefer to squat over the man's body with her knees resting on either side of his body. In this way she can raise her body so that she is almost sitting up if she desires. Sometimes a woman will alternate the way her body is placed while they are having intercourse in order to change the angle or depth of penetration. After finding a position she chooses, the woman (or man) inserts the penis into her vagina and begins to move in a way that pleases both partners.

Like any sexual position, this one has pros and cons.

Pros

- This is a terrific position for female arousal because it gives her so much control. She controls the angle at which the penis is inserted as well as the depth of penetration. She is also more in charge of the pace and speed of intercourse—as slow or fast as she likes.
- It is easy to maintain eye contact and intimacy.
- There can be full-body contact if the partners prefer.
- It is easy for either partner to caress the other's body, nipples, etc.
- It allows for intermittent deep kissing.
- The woman can touch and stimulate her clitoris to bring about or increase pleasure in her orgasm. The man can also

easily use his hands on her clitoris if this is what the partners prefer.

- This has often been considered a "bad girl" position (think
  Sharon Stone in *Basic Instinct*) and for that reason may be
  especially arousing.

Cons

- Some men are not comfortable with the woman appearing
  dominant or aggressive.

- Some women are equally uncomfortable with appearing or
  feeling aggressive.

- Some women are self-conscious about the way their faces
  sag down in this position, particularly if they already have a
  few wrinkles.

- Many women worry that their breasts and bodies sag, jig-
  gle, and droop too much for this position.

For women who have never fully explored the benefits of this position
and have insecurities about their bodies, I suggest starting out in a room
that is darkened or only dimly lit and practice becoming uninhibited.

side by side

Both partners lie facing each other, and one person puts a leg over
the other's hip. There are several variations. In one of them, which I
call the scissors position, the man lies on his side, while his partner
remains on her back perpendicular to him. The couple interweaves
their legs so their genitals meet.

Pros

This is a very relaxing position that doesn't require either person to support his or her body weight. Many people find that this is a great position first thing in the morning, when neither partner is in a mood for major acrobatics. I call this the "let's-just-put-it-in-and-see-if-anything-happens" position.

Many women like the eye contact and sense of intimacy that this position provides. With a couple of small body adjustments, it allows for the possibility of a man sucking and kissing a woman's breasts while having sex. The scissors variation also lets the man stimulate his partner's clitoris while he is inside her. Or, if the couple prefers, a woman can stimulate herself while the man continues stroking inside her vagina with his penis. The side-to-side position is sometimes recommended for pregnancy or for people with physical problems like arthritis.

Cons

This tends to be the least genitally stimulating position for both sexes because it is so relaxing. Frequently, there is not that much depth of penetration in this position and it is generally not stimulating to the G spot or the cul de sac.

rear entry

In the basic rear-entry position, the woman kneels on the bed on all fours, while the man kneels behind her. There are several variations, of course. The variation that I recommend is one in which the woman kneels at the edge of the bed with her butt in the air; in this position, she puts her arms folded down on the bed so that she can rest her head on them. This is a position that pushes emotional buttons in a lot of people: some love it; others dislike it.

Pros

- This position feels primitive and animalistic, an exciting turn-on for many people.

- This position is the best for fast stroking and depth of penetration; it's also great if the woman likes to have her cervix stimulated. This position is also one of the best ways for the penis to make contact with a woman's G spot.

- While in this position, if a woman chooses, she can shift her arms and hands so that she can easily stimulate her clitoris.

Cons

- The primitive and animalistic nature of this position can turn some people off.

- Some women (and a few men) say that this position feels too impersonal. They miss kissing and eye contact and complain that it provides little or no sense of intimacy or bonding.

- Many women feel that their butts look too wide and that their breasts hang down in an unattractive manner.

the vase or butterfly position

This is a variation of the man-on-top missionary position. I think it's worth describing on its own because it can have amazing results in the female orgasm department. (I call this the "vase" position because of the old joke about the good-looking woman who receives a big bouquet of roses on Valentine's Day, and her jealous co-worker says, "Well, you can be sure that if my boyfriend sent me such expensive flowers, I'd spend the next week on my back with my knees behind my shoulders." The other woman says, "Why? Don't you have a vase?" The position is sometimes identified by other names, for instance, *Cosmopolitan* magazine calls it the butterfly position.

In this position the woman lies on her back, tilts her pelvis, and puts her legs as far back as is possible without being uncomfortable. Depending on how flexible she is, she can put her knees on her shoulders or bend them so her vagina is opened wide. If she is flexible enough to put her knees behind her shoulders, all the better. This is best because at this angle, her vagina points almost straight up. Sometimes putting a pillow under her hips helps.

The man kneels between her legs so he doesn't have to support his weight with his arms and inserts his penis.

Pros

This position has several pluses for a woman:

- From this position, the vagina curves and is somewhat shortened. This position helps her uterus move off the vagina. Because of this, the man's penis is able to penetrate deeper and stimulate the G spot, the A spot, the cervix, and the cul de sac. If your partner wants a vaginal or uterine orgasm, this is the position to try.

- This position gives the man greater control of the depth of penetration. He can use his penis to switch back and forth between internal strokes and using his penis to caress her clitoris. It also allows the man to use his penis to tease the woman's PC muscle. Some women say that when they are very aroused, if their partner just teases the PC muscle by stroking gently with a little shallow penetration, it will trigger an orgasm.

- Because the woman's legs are spread, there is also great stimulation of the clitoris.

- This is a face-to-face position that allows plenty of eye contact.

- It's possible to kiss when the man leans forward.

- Both partners can see each other, and both partners can see the penis going in and out of the vagina. This gives the man his own personal porno movie view of his penis going in and out of her vagina.

- It's easy for the partners to gauge each other's level of arousal in this position.

- The man doesn't have to support his weight on his arms, elbow, or chest, which will help him last longer.

- This is also a good position for a man to practice multiple-orgasm techniques.

Cons

This is such a great position that I can't really think of any.

HOW LONG SHOULD INTERCOURSE LAST?

Bob, who just started dating after a divorce, says that he is still not sure how long intercourse should last, despite being married for five years. All he knows is that women complain if lovemaking is for too short a time, and sometimes they complain if it lasts too long.

Bob in not alone in his confusion. Many people have the same question. They want to know more about the sexual behavior of the so-called "average couple." How long do most people last? How long should it last? How long could it last? These questions aren't as easy to answer as it might seem because most surveys ask the question in the following form: *How long does a lovemaking session last from start to finish?* The answer to that is about half an hour to an hour on average. But that answer, of course, includes all aspects of a lovemaking session and does not refer specifically to intercourse.

It's possible to get a historical perspective on sex by looking at some old statistics. The famous Kinsey Report, *Sexual Behavior in the Human Male,* was published in 1948 and was considered very shocking at the time. The men Dr. Alfred Kinsey interviewed reported that they averaged two to three minutes in sexual intercourse. When I look at that statistic now, my initial reaction is one of disbelief. More recent sex surveys taken in the 1990s indicate that men last on an average of six to seven minutes. That means that the time the "average" man spent having intercourse actually doubled or sometimes tripled in the intervening fifty-plus years. That six or seven minutes is still not too impressive if you consider the following: When men are surveyed about how long they would *like* intercourse to last, the average response is fifteen to twenty minutes.

Nonetheless, it's interesting to think about the reasons why men are now lasting longer than they used to. I assume it is the influence of the sexual revolution and the women's movement. Unlike the women in Kinsey's era, women today expect orgasms during intercourse, so they encourage men to last longer. Today, both men and women have higher expectations of sexual intercourse. Women want to maintain the intimate sexual connection for longer periods, and men want to be able to please and satisfy their partners.

When men try to last longer during intercourse, they are basically fighting against thousands of years of evolution because all mammals have evolved to ejaculate rather quickly. If most women were to think about this, I think we would all acknowledge that we totally applaud and appreciate this effort.

Men want to know how to last longer, and this is a good thing, but when it comes to telling men how to sustain their erections for longer periods of time, I realize that there is a great deal of questionable advice out there. Guys start hearing this stuff when they are in junior high so let's discuss some of the things that do and don't help a man maintain an erection for a longer period of time.

INEFFECTIVE STRATEGIES FOR LASTING LONGER

Go Out and Buy a Cream That Claims to Numb the Penis

Well, in truth, these creams probably do numb the penis, but they also numb the vagina. No fun for either partner.

Think About Something Other Than Sex

This is probably the most common advice that men are given. They are told to ignore what they are feeling and start thinking about baseball scores, math problems, and home repair projects. It's amazing that so many men have tried to follow this advice, which may work temporarily, but it's not a real solution. If you struggle to ignore and push aside all those wonderful sensations you are feeling during sex, you will a) have less enjoyment, and b) never get any sense of control. You'll always feel like you are skating on thin ice. You can only learn to control that which you accept.

Have a Few Drinks

Liquor may slow down your responses somewhat, and for that reason, you may last a little longer, but it's not a real solution. The reason alcohol works in the short term is because it slows down all of your reflexes, including your ejaculatory reflex. If you habitually rely on alcohol to last longer, without discussing what you are doing to your health, you will need more drinks each time. Plus, if you then have sex sober, you could experience rebound premature ejaculation, which is a reflex ejaculation without an orgasm, and sometimes without even an erection. This is very scary.

Use a Condom

Yes, when you wear a condom, you don't feel as much. Therefore, it stands to reason that you will last longer. But the same thing applies as with alcohol: When you have intercourse without a condom, chances are you'll ejaculate even faster than you did before.

Take Antidepressants

It's true that using selective serotonin reuptake inhibitors (SSRIs) like Prozac, Zoloft, and Paxil might make you last longer before you ejaculate. In fact, drugs such as these have been shown to be effective for staying power. But you know what? I wouldn't go there! I would consider using drugs like these to prolong your erections to be overkill and a last resort. There are many potential side effects. It's also a fact that while these drugs can delay ejaculation, they can also lower your libido and interfere with orgasms.

Masturbate Before You Go on a Date to Take the "Edge" Off

We all have an image of a guy about to go out on the famous "third" date with the girl of his dreams. He's positive they are going to end up in bed and he really wants to impress her with his staying power, so he masturbates quickly before he leaves the house. You're not going on a date with a loaded gun in your pants, are you? This solution can really backfire on you, no pun intended. When you masturbate quickly before a date, you are laying the groundwork for a massive problem with premature ejaculation. Every time you masturbate quickly, it conditions your body to ejaculate that much quicker the next time. There is another problem with this approach: Masturbating will take the edge off and you might indeed last longer, but it will also take the edge off your passion, and it's possible that your partner will feel the difference.

GOOD STRATEGIES FOR LASTING LONGER

Some Positions Will Help You Last Longer

This is true. In general, most men last longer in the side-to-side, butterfly, and female superior positions than they do in the male superior or rear entry positions.

Self-Awareness Will Help You Last Longerr

This is one of the best pieces of advice I can give any man who wants to make his erection last longer. If you really know yourself and are conscious and aware of how you respond sexually, you have a much better chance of figuring out what's happening.

Some men, for example, don't last as long as they would like during sex because they aren't having as much sex as their bodies require. These guys are always a hair trigger away from ejaculation. Try to be aware of your sexual needs and how often you have an uncontrollable urge to ejaculate. For some men, particularly young ones, this is several times a day. For others, it's once a day, twice a week, once a week, once a month, or whatever. This is not about being a statistic. It's about you and your sexuality. If you are not having intercourse at your desired level of frequency, masturbate in between. Use the peaking lessons to help you last longer so that you will be in total control of your erection when you are having sex with a partner.

Be aware of the changes your body experiences. As you get older, you will feel the need to ejaculate less frequently. Don't force yourself to ejaculate a certain number of times a week because that's what you did when you were twenty. Be aware of your own body and its needs. I sometimes talk to women who are in sexual relationships with men who insist upon trying, and I do mean trying, to have sex as often as they did when they were kids. Even with the help of Viagra, this is probably going to end up being an unsatisfactory and frustrating experience.

Be aware of what is happening while you are having sex with a partner. Start paying attention to everything that you are feeling during intercourse. Focus on what your penis is experiencing and how her vagina feels; enjoy all the subtle as well as intense sensations. Be aware of the various elements of your lovemaking as it is happening. This will help you slow down and be more in the moment.

Practice Peaking

Reread the peaking exercises on pages 44–45. Practicing during masturbation and then doing these with a partner will show you how to let your arousal go up and down in that wave or peak-like pattern. This is the best way to learn to last longer. Once you have these exercises under control, you will never feel like you're fighting to keep from ejaculating.

Squeezing Your PC Muscle

If you squeeze your PC muscle when you are highly aroused, it will often take your arousal down a notch. By the way, this is different than using your PC muscle to hold back your ejaculation and experience male multiple orgasm. Don't use your PC muscle to slow down unless you have a very firm erection; otherwise you could lose the erection. This is something else you might want to practice alone during masturbation so you get more awareness of your body and in the process gain greater control.

A WORD OF CAUTION: Don't try to hold back an ejaculation. This is not the same as having control through awareness and peaking. If you hold back an ejaculation without having done your awareness and peaking exercises, you will probably be holding it back by unconsciously squeezing your PC muscle really hard. This is how you can get really sore testicles, which used to be known in high schools across the country as "blue balls." This practice will also interfere with your learning to focus on your sensations and can sometimes contribute to overly rapid ejaculation as well as erection problems.

MAKING SEX MORE INTIMATE AND EROTIC

Intercourse is still the most intimate thing two people can do together. Sex is better when all the elements of passion and affection come together. Remember that your partner likes having sex with you because she likes you. It's a rare woman who doesn't want to be stroked, kissed, and touched during intercourse. Kissing deepens and heightens the sensual experience. Passion when it is expressed has the power to intensify and electrify sex. Let your partner know what you are feeling. You can do it with your eyes, your mouth, your hands, and your words. Tell her what you like about having sex with her; tell her how she makes you feel. You don't have to talk nonstop, but a few well-chosen and sincere phrases are a big turn-on. Let her feel your excitement. Your passion encourages her to be more open with her own.

Don't forget to make eye contact. It's exciting for both partners to gaze into each other's eyes and share what they are experiencing.

SEX IN UNUSUAL LOCATIONS

One of my friends had a boyfriend, let's call him Derek. Well, Derek lived about a block from the beach, and he had this fantasy about having sex on a starlit night, lying on a blanket on the sand. I think he said something about wanting to hear the waves crashing to the shore while he had an orgasm. His fantasy wasn't as easy to accommodate as one might think. For one thing, the water line at high tide was too close to the road to provide enough privacy. But, sure enough, one starry, starry night my friend was visiting Derek during low tide, and he convinced her to head for the beach. They took a blanket and found a spot behind a rock. Now everyone who has ever been to the beach knows that sand always gets on the blanket, no matter what you do. They also know that sand looks a lot softer and more inviting than it really is. My friend said that what she remembers from that night is a 200-pound guy pounding into her on a hard surface with sand getting in her crotch and no-see-ums chewing up her ankles. She hated it. Derek seemed to enjoy himself, even though he got bit on the butt. Nonetheless, the next time Derek suggested the beach, my friend said, "Forget about it."

Somebody else I know said she once had sex in a cow pasture in Hawaii and that it was okay, except for the smell and the flies. Lots of men and women I know have had sex on the living room rug, with or without a romantic fireplace, and they had the rug burn on their butts and knees to prove it. I personally have a scar from one such session permanently embossed on my lower back. I haven't been too success-ful at having sex in exotic locales and am suggesting that a place that seems like it would be a real turn-on doesn't always work out that way.

Another friend recently told me that she was down in the Bahamas recently. She was trying to get into a dinghy tied up to a dock when she spotted a couple nearby obviously having sex in the water. She was startled, which made her miss her footing, and she crashed into the water as well as into the couple. I guess she was less disruptive to them than a wide variety of other things could have been. One friend tried having sex in the Atlantic Ocean while vaca-tioning in the Hamptons, and her boyfriend's bathing suit took off with the tide. This was the only article of clothing he had with him.

I'm also not a big fan of sex in hot tubs, showers, or pools. Chlorine can dry out delicate vaginal tissues, and some of the spa chemicals can trigger a vaginal infection. If you're a fan of having sex outside (and I am), I think your best bet is to figure out how to cre-ate a private area outside your house. Perhaps a screened-in patio or deck that you can outfit with futons or comfy lounge chairs, none of those cross-ribbed plastic numbers.

The success of sex in exotic locations is at least somewhat dependent on who you are and who you are with. It helps if you are both young and agile and without major allergies to grass, mosqui-toes, pollen, etc.

CUDDLING AND PILLOW TALK AFTER SEX

You don't really need to have me tell you that women love to cuddle after sex, now do you? Cuddling is good; cuddling is cozy; cuddling is one of the best ways to bond and deepen your connection with each other.

Women also like it when you tell them that you liked having sex with them. You can say something simple like, "That was terrific!" However, you cannot say that as you turn your total attention to the TV remote or your dog. If you want to mumble only a few words along these lines, mumble them into her ear while you are nuzzling her neck. Keep your voice throaty and intimate as opposed to casual. Don't make it sound like you both just enjoyed a game of pick-up ball together and are now wandering off into your everyday world where you barely know each other. If you want to get more specific about what you liked, all the better.

Women hate it when their partners immediately detach after sex and act as though they barely know the woman with whom they just shared such intimacy. That's one of the reasons why they like to cuddle after sex. Napping is okay, but don't roll over to do it. Keep her snuggled in your arms for at least a while. Before you disentangle your bodies to roll over and go to sleep or get out of bed, a sweet and affectionate hug is always a good thing.

As you are getting out of bed or falling asleep, consider giving her a loving kiss. It doesn't have to be on the lips. You can kiss her anywhere. Some favorite spots include the neck, the hand, and the tummy. If you feel this way, this is always a good time to say, "I love you," or even, "I loved watching you have an orgasm," or anything else that acknowledges the connection.

chapter seven

BECOME AN ORGASM EXPERT

As we become more and more sexually aroused, blood begins to flow into the genitals, which become significantly more swollen and enlarged. Heart rate, blood pressure, and muscle tension increase. Your heart rate can temporarily reach a peak between 150 and 180 beats a minute. In many people, orgasm includes uncontrollable spasms of the long muscles in the arms and the legs. The orgasmic reflex occurs when all that collected tension is dispersed. For both men and women, the main change that occurs during orgasm is that the pubococcygeus (PC) muscle begins to spasm rhythmically. In women, these PC muscle spasms are usually felt around the opening of the vagina. In men, the PC muscle spasms cause ejaculation.

For most of us, orgasm is an intensely pleasurable experience that includes physical and psychological feelings of relief or release. Many people experience a spiritual component to their orgasm that includes a feeling of transcendence; some go so far as to say that they almost enter into an altered state of consciousness. Many men and women particularly enjoy orgasm because it gives them a stronger sense of connection and intimacy with their partners. Some men and women, however, have idiosyncratic reactions such as sadness or uncontrollable weeping or even sweating.

Statistically speaking, men's orgasms are more reliable. This is sometimes called the orgasm gap.

THE UNIVERSAL MALE QUESTION: IS SHE FAKING IT?

Jake thinks that he and his girlfriend Brianna have great sex. He says that she rocks his world, and he *thinks* that he does the same for her. He knows that she is attracted to him; he knows that she is aroused by him; and he knows that she loves him. What he doesn't know for sure is whether or not she is having orgasms. Jake has two older sisters. He used to lie awake nights with his ear pressed against a glass on his bedroom wall to hear them talk. He absolutely knows that women lie about orgasms. Could Brianna be lying to him? Could she just be making all the right sounds? What is it with women and orgasms?

If two people, a man and a woman, are having sex together, and you had to bet on which one of them was more likely to have an orgasm, which one should you bet on? You don't have to be a student of human sexuality to know that the right answer is the man.

Most men, no matter how sexually experienced or sophisticated they might be, are still confused about women and orgasms. There is a good reason for this because so much information about women and orgasms has been confusing and sometimes just plain wrong. As a result, the average guy is still left with two main concerns.

How can I make sure she has an orgasm?

How can I know for sure that she did?

In order to answer these questions fully, I'd like to give you some background on women and orgasms. Hundreds of years ago, before people fully understood how conception works, many thought that a woman's orgasm was as necessary as a man's in order for conception to occur. This all changed during the Victorian era when it was considered unseemly for a woman to even want any kind of sexual gratification. Those women who did have orgasms were often too embarrassed to admit it. There was some belief, however, among physicians that an orgasm was a medical treatment—just what the doctor ordered—for stressed women and a condition that was clinically known as hysteria. More than a few women went to the doctor's office to receive clitoral stimulation. Fortunately, Victorian attitudes have changed, but even so, the female orgasm continues to be a source of confusion.

For many years, it was thought that female orgasms were divided into two types: clitoral and vaginal. This was primarily because of the influence of Sigmund Freud. Freud noted that most women reported that they could have an orgasm from manual stimulation of the clitoris, but there were some women who reported orgasms that felt like they came from deep inside the vagina during intercourse. Freud then jumped to an erroneous conclusion that influenced all those interested in the study of human sexuality.

Aware that a young girl could reach orgasm by rubbing her clitoris, Freud dubbed clitoral orgasms as immature or basically inferior. He taught that only a psychologically mature woman could have a vaginal orgasm during intercourse. Freudians then took this one step further by decreeing that if an adult woman still had to rely on touching her clitoris for orgasms, that was a sign that she was fixated at an immature stage of sexual development. Until the women's movement and sexual revolution of the 1960s and 1970s, that is honestly what people believed. Many psychologically savvy women of that time period were embarrassed to acknowledge that they had clitoral orgasms because that would imply that they were somehow lacking in "womanliness."

With the sexual revolution and the women's movement, Freud's statements about women's orgasms began to be questioned, and suddenly clitoral orgasms were back in style. In fact, the work of Masters and Johnson, two pioneering sex researchers of the 1960s and 1970s, indicated that all women's orgasms were clitoral. In the early 1970s, researchers also began to talk about blended orgasms (which sounds like a great name for a cocktail); they said that this type of orgasm could occur if women had intercourse while they *also* stimulated the clitoris.

During Freud's day and even during the early 1970s, we didn't know a whole lot about female sexual anatomy. We now know that there are at least two nerve pathways to orgasm for women. Stimulation of the clitoris travels to the spinal cord via the pudendal nerve, whereas stimulation of the deepest part of the vagina travels to the spinal cord via the pelvic nerve. All this means is that what women have been saying is true: The same woman can have all different kinds of orgasms.

THE DIFFERENCE BETWEEN MALE AND FEMALE ORGASMS

There are some major differences between men and women when it comes to orgasm. Men's orgasms are pretty much connected to the stimulation of the penis. A woman's orgasmic ability is much more diffuse. That means the following:

- A woman is more likely to be able to have multiple orgasms.
- Women are more likely to have orgasms as a result of being emotionally and mentally aroused, without any physical touch.
- There are more places on a woman's body that, with stimulation, can trigger orgasms.

Here is a list of some of the genital sites that can trigger a female orgasm.

external genital sites

Clitoris

The clitoris contains erectile tissue and becomes hard and swollen when it is stimulated. For a majority of women, stimulation of the clitoris is "Old Faithful" and the way to orgasm that never fails.

Inner and Outer Vaginal Lips

Some women report that pressure or stimulation of this site is part and parcel of their orgasmic experience.

Urethral Opening (the U Spot)

Although this particular spot can be painfully sensitive for some women, others say that stimulating it can cause an orgasm. An important thing to remember about the urethral opening is that it is easily irritated. A word of warning: Treat this area gently and never try to put objects in the urethra.

Vaginal Opening/PC Muscle

Women who have been busy doing their PC exercises know that a strong PC muscle can keep the vagina tight and increase muscle mass. This increases sensations of pleasure and release. Some women report that they can have orgasms simply by stimulating the PC muscle.

internal genital sites

Grafenberg Spot (G Spot)

The famous and infamously elusive G spot is found on the front wall of the vagina about two thirds of the way in. Some researchers believe that the G spot is responsible for all vaginal orgasms. When the G spot has not been stimulated, it's very small and soft. For this reason, it's easier to find when the woman is excited. When a woman is aroused, the G spot, which also contains erectile tissue, fills with blood and swells considerably. Women may find it easier to reach their G spot on their own by using a dildo. A woman's partner can usually locate the G spot by inserting a finger all the way into the vagina and then hooking the finger toward the front, in the direction of the woman's tummy. The first few times, it might be easier to find when a woman is lying on her stomach. For some women rubbing this area produces an intensely pleasurably orgasm; other women merely report pleasure without orgasm; and a few women say that when it is stimulated, they feel little or nothing. A woman who wants to use her own hands for exploration might try squatting in order to locate it.

Anterior Fornix (A Spot)

The A spot is a spongy area that is also located on the front wall of the vagina a little beyond the G spot and before the cervix. It's so close to the G spot that it's almost impossible to stimulate one without the other. Newest research indicates that the A spot holds the secret to vaginal lubrication.

Cervix

The cervix, which is about three quarters of the way back in the vaginal canal, provides the opening to the uterus. It's easy to feel because it is firm and protrudes. Some women find thrusting against the cervix painful. Others describe it as pleasurable (see below).

Cul de Sac

The cul de sac (sometimes also called the Pouch of Douglas, which kind of makes you wonder who Douglas was) has only recently started to receive any serious attention. It is located at the end of the vagina behind the cervix. When a woman is strongly aroused, the uterus tightens and lifts up, exposing the area known as the cul de sac.

Combination Internal and External Trigger (the Paraurethral Sponge)

When a woman is sexually aroused, there is an entire genital area that becomes swollen and hypersensitive. Imagine cupping your hand around a woman's genitals while your finger is inserted into the vagina. This is the part of the female anatomy known as the paraurethral sponge. Many women have orgasms when both internal and external triggers located in this area are stimulated simultaneously.

other places that have been associated with female orgasm

Some women have reported having orgasms even when the genitals have not been stimulated. There is evidence that some women can reach orgasm when their breasts are stimulated. Some women have reported that when their nipples are being sucked, it feels as though there is a direct connection to the clitoris. Women have also reported experiencing orgasm from mouth kissing, or being touched on the neck or face. In addition, some women have said that they had orgasms from reading erotic literature, without touching themselves, or even from dreams or fantasies. Stimulation of the feet does it for some women, and I've heard women say that the right man sucking their toes can bring them to orgasm. I've also known women who report having had orgasms while doing oral sex on a man.

WHY WOMEN HAVE PROBLEMS WITH ORGASM

So with all this information about women's orgasms being diffuse, and all these different areas on a woman's body that can trigger orgasm, why aren't more women having orgasms? Why aren't they having them more easily? And why don't they always have them during intercourse?

What's the number one reason a woman has problems with orgasm?

The main reason a woman has difficulty reaching orgasm is that she doesn't have enough experience masturbating all by herself. Some men assume that the right man can bring any woman to orgasm. It's a nice myth, but it's not really true. In order to have orgasms, a woman has to know how to have them. She has to know what kind of stimulation and on what part of her body will bring her to orgasm. Masturbation is how a woman teaches herself what works and what doesn't. This is how she can get the experience she needs. Women who have a history of masturbating and bringing themselves to orgasm as adolescents tend to be more orgasmic with their partners later in life.

Many young women experience intercourse or oral sex with a partner before they ever masturbate. This is especially true with young girls who begin sexual activity with a partner when they are still in their early teens. There are young women who have never even touched themselves or explored their own genitals. How can these women know how to position their bodies? How can they know how to guide a lover? I did a class survey recently and about 20 percent of the women told me that they were sexually active with partners, but had never had orgasms.

These women need to explore their own bodies; in this way, they will learn how to go from arousal to orgasm with a partner. Some men feel threatened if they learn that their partners are pleasuring themselves, either with their hands or by using a vibrator or dildo. I always tell men to relax and advise them to encourage their partners in self-exploration. A woman who knows her own body will inevitably be the better lover.

orgasm expectations get in the way

Faulty expectations are another reason why women have trouble with orgasms. Some women have read descriptions of orgasms that include fireworks, violins, waves crashing on the shoreline, and even angels singing. When Masters and Johnson did their research and lab studies, they needed to assign a standard by which they could define and recognize female orgasm. Therefore, by their determination, a woman had an orgasm if her heart rate went up and she experienced spasms in her PC muscle. This response can indicate a very weak orgasm. When a woman experiences an orgasm like this, particularly if it's her very first orgasm, she can be totally underwhelmed. She might even miss it. A typical reaction might be, "That's the Big O everybody talks about? Is that all there is? It's hardly worth it!"

Low expectations are also a problem. This is that old orgasm gap again. Some women simply believe that either they'll never have one or that they can only have them through masturbation and that they'll never have one with a partner. This is a negative attitude that I totally reject. I believe that every person's body is capable of orgasm and that every person is capable of orgasm with a partner, provided that there is sufficient arousal and the right stimulation.

ORGASM TROUBLESHOOTING

Students ask me many questions about women and orgasm. Here are some of the most common:

My girlfriend has orgasms some of the time from intercourse, but not all the time. I have no idea why. Do you have any suggestions?

This usually happens because the man and woman are at vastly different arousal levels when sex begins. Think of arousal on a 1–10 scale as described previously in the peaking exercises. Many times, when the couple starts having intercourse, the man may already be at level #7–8, but the woman hasn't quite caught up. She may have already had an orgasm from oral sex; she may just have a harder time shifting gears from the rest of her life; she may be distracted because she is thinking about work or even a chocolate soufflé that she's planning to make for you for dessert. The best advice here is to try to make sure that she's at a high level of arousal *before* you start intercourse.

So how can a man tell if a woman is aroused?

Here's another way that men and women are totally different. A man's physical and psychological arousal are usually pretty much in sync. If a man has an erection, and you ask him how psychologically aroused he is, he'll think you're nuts. He'll say, "Of course I'm aroused, look at this boner!"

Believe it or not, a woman's physical arousal and psychological arousal can be at completely different levels. When a woman is physically aroused, her vagina lubricates, her breasts swell, her face may flush, her heart rate increases, she breathes faster, and her voice gets lower.

Some men say that they have learned to insert a finger in their partner's vagina to see whether or not she is fully lubricated. I know that some people advise this; however, I don't think that lubrication is always a reliable indicator. It's entirely possible for a woman to be lubricating without the rest of her quite catching up. If you were to ask her if she was aroused, she might say no. And she would mean it. She wouldn't be in denial or lying or jerking you around. No matter what her level or lubrication, she may still not be psychologically turned on.

There are other reasons why you can't depend on the amount of lubrication in her vagina to tell you what you need to know. You may have already had oral sex, or you may have been stimulating her with your hands. Both of these can use up her natural lubrication. If this happens, she could be very aroused yet lack lubrication.

Levels of lubrication also vary in women depending on their age and hormone levels. A woman over forty can be totally aroused and have minimal lubrication. Something else to consider is whether or not the lubrication you are feeling is hers naturally. Remember that lubrication might be part and parcel of the method of birth control you are using. All the forms of spermicide jellies and gels, for example, add lubrication to the vagina. Some women just automatically add a little lubrication when they think they might be going to have sex. In short, she could feel very well lubricated and still not be completely aroused.

A more reliable gauge of female arousal is clitoral enlargement and swelling of the paraurethral sponge. Can you hear her heart? Is it beating faster? How about the tone of her voice? When a woman is fully aroused, she doesn't want her body to be separated from the person who is giving her pleasure. Does your partner act as though her body is glued to yours? If you move away slightly, does she automatically move with you? How about her breathing?

The best way to tell if a woman is fully aroused is to ask her. You don't have to ask her while you are having sex, but you could. Another way to find out more about your partner and her arousal is to ask her at a completely different time. Some night when you're sitting on the couch and talking, tell her that you want to know more about her, and ask her what she feels when she is aroused. Find out how she describes the difference between physical and psychological arousal and how she knows when it is all coming together in the right way. Ask her to tell you the next time you have sex.

She can have an orgasm when I touch her or when we have oral sex, but not with intercourse—in any position. What's up?

Sometimes I'll talk to a guy who wonders why his girlfriend can't have an orgasm with intercourse. Often he and his partner have tried just about every position. They have tried it with him on his back, her on her back, standing, sitting, on a table, against a chair, and so on. Nothing has worked.

Most of the time, when a woman can't have an orgasm from intercourse, the biggest problem is the strength of the PC muscle that surrounds the opening of the vagina. When a woman has an orgasm, that muscle spasms and contracts. What she is experiencing is a sensation that feels like her vagina is opening and closing really fast. If a woman's PC muscle isn't in very good shape, it's harder for it to spasm when something is in her vagina. It's just physically more difficult for that PC muscle to tighten around an object that's filling the vagina.

The solution for this can be a simple one: PC muscle exercises! I usually recommend the advanced ones where a woman tightens her muscle for ten seconds and then loosens for ten seconds. Some women even say that they can trigger an orgasm on their own in this way while doing their PC exercises. After a woman does these for a few weeks, she can begin practicing the exercise with a dildo inserted.

If you are having sex, suggest that she practice the exercise by squeezing her PC muscle around your penis when you have intercourse. Most men love this sensation.

I read somewhere that if a woman is going to have an orgasm during intercourse, it's going to happen within a certain time period. Is this true?

Many men have heard about the seven-minute myth of female orgasm. The seven-minute rule says that if a woman is going to have an orgasm during intercourse, on average, she'll have it within seven minutes of starting intercourse. I believe this rule originated in some sexual research, and it may even have some truth to it. I mean, it sounds plausible. The problem is how people have interpreted it. Many people have interpreted this to mean that the longer a man lasts in intercourse, the more likely the woman is to have an orgasm, and that's not true.

The key to understanding the seven-minute myth and making it work for you is to pay attention to the first part of the statement: "If a woman is going to have an orgasm from intercourse. . . ." This whole approach only applies to women who are going to have orgasm with intercourse. For women who have difficulty reaching orgasm with intercourse, you could last all night, and the chances are that she is still not going to come.

My girlfriend is having trouble with orgasms. She had a traumatic event in her family last year and is currently taking an antidepressant. We both wonder if this could be interfering with her orgasms.

Some antidepressants are more likely to inhibit orgasm than others. Psychiatrists have been more likely to focus on the male orgasm response in relation to these drugs. That's because it's so much more obvious when a man fails to come, and men are also much more likely to visit a doctor to complain. There are other medications which may work without affecting orgasm, and a visit to the doctor is in order.

My wife swears that she is more sensitive on one side of her clitoris and vagina than the other. Is that possible? She also has no difficulty having orgasms at night, but in the morning, forget it. She says she's less sensitive before noon.

Many women say that they seem to have more nerve endings on one side of the vagina or the clitoris than the other. I know it seems strange, but I've heard this so often that I don't doubt the truth in this. A study done in the 1950s showed huge variations in the way nerve endings are distributed in different women's genitals. While most women have a lot of nerve endings on the clitoris, some women have a lot in the inner and out lips so it shouldn't be surprising that some women report that they have more sensation on one side or the other.

The same kind of thing is true of sex at different times of the day. Many women say that if they are going to have an orgasm it's going to happen in the morning; others say just the opposite. This is the kind of thing that a woman is likely to know about herself.

HOW TO TELL IF SHE HAS AN ORGASM

If she starts trembling and yells, "Oh my God, I'm coming!" you're probably in good shape. If not, you need to know a little bit about women's physiology. When a woman has an orgasm, two things happen. Her PC muscle will spasm a few times, and her heart rate goes up very quickly and flutters. A woman's PC muscle surrounds the opening of the vagina so if you are doing oral sex by imitating shallow intercourse, you will be in a position to feel it if her muscle spasms. If you are doing oral sex on her clitoris, you might use your hand to press lightly on the PC muscle or you can insert one or two fingers into the vagina. Either way, you will feel the spasms. You can also use a hand to caress her breasts and feel her heart rate increase.

Another thing that can happen when a woman has an orgasm is that her vagina will suck in air. When her muscles spasm, the air will blow back out and make a noise. This is a fairly reliable sign that a woman is having an orgasm.

When a woman has an orgasm from stimulation of the cul de sac, the orgasm can be fairly dramatic. Her legs may shake and her breathing will sound almost like panting, choking, or gulping. After this kind of orgasm, a woman may say that she feels weak in the knees if she tries to stand up.

WHAT MASTERS AND JOHNSON DIDN'T KNOW ABOUT FEMALE ORGASM

Almost forty years ago, when Masters and Johnson first announced that all female orgasms are the result of direct or indirect stimulation of the clitoris, many women breathed a huge sigh of relief. It was as if women were finally given permission to do something they had been doing all along. I think the majority of men quickly jumped on the bandwagon. Most of them wanted to give their partners orgasms, and they were all too eager to start licking, sucking, kissing, touching, and stroking.

But we now know that there are many sensitive sites within the vagina that can bring a woman to orgasm. If you want to be the lover every woman dreams of, my suggestion is that at least every now and then, you should ignore her clitoris. That's right: *ignore the clitoris*! Remember, as much as she may enjoy having you stimulate her clitoris, she can do this for herself any old time she wants. What you can do is use your penis to stimulate all of her sensitive vaginal areas during intercourse. Here's how to do this.

Start by using a variation of the butterfly position. Have your partner lie on her back and put a pillow under her butt so she is comfortable with her legs bent just slightly back. Kneel in front of her, straight up, with your weight on your knees. You're going to use your penis to explore and probe her vagina. Your penis has the power to make your partner totally aroused and satisfied. Here's how:

If you were able to look into a vagina, you would see that it looks like a tunnel with ridges or corrugated areas running up and down the sides. When you insert your penis, start stroking very slowly. See if you can feel these ridges. Now try to angle your penis so that it stimulates the G spot and the A spot. Remember, these are on the front vaginal wall, facing you. From your kneeling position you should have the control you need to do this. Ask your partner to tilt her hips so that she can feel what your penis is doing.

Stroke along the front wall of her vagina slowly. Do this for a few minutes and see if you can feel the tissue in her vagina start to swell and lubricate. Remember to go slowly. Gaze into your partner's eyes, and ask her to tell you if she is having sensations in her vagina. In this position, at least one of your hands is free. Every now and then, use it to increase the bond and the feeling of connection between you. Stroke her thighs; lean down briefly and use your hands to caress her breasts or touch her face. Lean down for just a moment and kiss. Tell her how much pleasure you get from looking at her breasts and her body. Tell her how excited she makes you.

Remember to go slowly as your penis explores her vagina. Very slowly. Let your penis tease and tempt her vagina. Can you tell by her breathing how excited she is becoming? Is she becoming flushed? Push your penis even farther into her vagina. Can you feel her cervix? You can do this by pointing your penis up and back. Do this to the right and to the left. The cervix in each woman is placed a little differently on one side or the other so take your time and explore her vagina.

Now lift your partner's butt off the bed. Spread her cheeks slightly and plunge as deeply into her vagina as you can. See if you can enter the cul de sac. The cul de sac is rich in nerve endings and capable of triggering the most explosive orgasm any woman can ever experience. Some women respond immediately almost as soon as a man's penis is able to penetrate the area. If this is the case with your partner, you can't help but feel her response. Continue stroking in and out and stimulating the deepest parts of your partner's vagina. Is she ready for orgasm?

Can your words help tip her over the edge? Tell her what you are feeling. Tell her how much you love being this deep in her vagina. Find the words and expressions that you know you are both comfortable using.

This may be the time to speed up your stroking. Notice how aroused your partner is becoming. Do you feel her excitement? How about your own? Are you almost ready for an orgasm?

As an interesting side note, a woman's sexual response is designed to help you reach orgasm. When she reaches the plateau phase of the sexual response cycle (that's about a level #8 on the arousal scale), the middle third of her vagina will often actually tighten up and grip your penis. If you feel this happening, it isn't your imagination. It is, however, your confirmation that she is fully aroused. Her vagina really is getting tighter; it really does seem to be holding your penis, and this actually does make your penis get bigger. Masters and Johnson called this the formation of the orgasmic platform. The purpose is to help you reach orgasm.

BLENDED ORGASMS

Jackie is like many other women: when she masturbates, she stimulates her clitoris with one hand. With the other, she inserts either a dildo or her fingers into her vagina. This method assures her of an orgasm within a matter of minutes. Also, like many other women, she has never told any of the men with whom she has had sex her preferred method of having orgasms. She keeps hoping that her current lover will figure it out on his own, but she doesn't know how to tell him.

If you are a man who has a girlfriend who seems to be having difficulty reaching orgasm with either clitoral stimulation or inter-course alone, you might want to think about ways that you can stim-ulate her clitoris while you are moving inside of her.

Here are some suggestions:

- You can stimulate her clitoris while you are in the butterfly position.
- Suggest that she stimulate her own clitoris while you are in any of the variations of the male superior position.
- You can stimulate her clitoris while you are lying side to side.
- You can stimulate her clitoris when she is on top of you. She can also do it herself.
- She can stimulate her own clitoris during any of the varia-tions of the rear entry position.

ORGASM LESSONS

Suppose you have tried all the above ways to make sure that your partner has an orgasm, and you are still not sure if it's working. What can you do? Let me tell you a true story about a woman friend, Joan, and a man named Richard. Joan started dating Richard a few years back, and although he was an exceptionally good and confident lover, Joan did not have orgasms with him. This wasn't unusual. Joan had never had orgasms with any man. Finally, one night after Richard had tried everything in his repertoire, to no avail, he said, "We need to talk."

Joan didn't know what to expect. Was he going to announce that he was fed up with their sexual relationship? She was completely surprised when he said, "You know what? I think you need orgasm lessons. And I'm going to give them to you." He was so good-natured and charming and confident that Joan could do nothing but smile.

They made a date for the following Saturday, and Joan didn't know what to expect. When Richard arrived, he had a dozen roses, a bottle of wine, and a wrapped cardboard box. "It's a present," Richard said. When Joan opened it, she was stunned when she saw a vibrator. "I figure," Richard said, as he kissed her, "that between this thing and me, we can figure out what we need to do so you can have an orgasm."

Joan told me that Richard managed to incorporate the vibrator into their lovemaking in such a way that it became a highly charged and sensual experience for both of them. And yes, she did have an orgasm.

She learned that she was one of many women who need clitoral stimulation combined with penetration to reach orgasm. Joan said that it was Richard's sense of confidence that made the biggest difference. Joan also said that she and Richard used the vibrator so much that they wore down the batteries, but by the time that happened, Joan had learned how to have orgasms in a wide variety of other ways.

buying your partner a dildo or vibrator

Playing with sex toys can be a lot of fun for the couple that wants to experiment and add another dimension to their lovemaking. I mention it here because dildos and/or vibrators can be extraordinarily helpful in teaching women how to become more orgasmic. If you want to get one for your partner, you should know the difference between them. Dildos, which are specifically shaped like penises, may or may not also be vibrators. Vibrators, which always vibrate, may or may not be shaped like penises.

If you are going to buy one, I would suggest looking for one that is both a vibrator and a dildo. Dildo-shaped vibrators come in different sizes. Find one that is shaped like a normal-sized penis. I also recommend one that is flexible so that it can be bent into a gooseneck shape; in this way, it can easily be used to stimulate the G spot. Also, try to get one that has at least two vibration settings, low and high.

Some women feel that they are often very close to orgasm, but then, just as it's about to happen, their partners move just a little or change the rhythm just a bit, and they feel as though they have to start all over again. The thing about vibrators is that they provide a consistent and constant vibration, which can be very helpful.

If you are going to use a vibrator against your partner's clitoris, remember to start out with very little pressure and the low setting. Hold the vibrator lightly but firmly. Ask your partner how it feels. Does she want more or less pressure? Keep experimenting until you get it right.

Don't be intimidated by your partner's vibrator! This is a very important piece of advice. Some men actually feel jealous or complain that the vibrator is taking their place. This is so much not the case. Trust me, a woman is not turned on by her vibrator. However, once she is aroused and responsive to you, a vibrator can help her reach orgasm. If she feels comfortable enough to allow you to use a vibrator during sex, she probably feels a level of sexual trust. A man who is confident enough to include a vibrator in his lovemaking is very appealing. Some men also find using a vibrator on a woman very sexy and exciting.

Another word of caution: Don't keep a vibrator in your home to be used with more than one woman. There is a risk of transmitting bacteria, and most women also hate this because it makes them feel less special.

FAKING IT!

When I took a survey of young women, several of them told me that they believed that all women fake it at least once in a while. A woman who fakes orgasm typically says that her main reason for doing so is to make it clear to her partner that he is pleasing her. Remember that the two infallible signs of an orgasm are PC muscle spasms and a rapid heart rate. If she doesn't have these, she didn't have an orgasm, but that doesn't mean that she didn't have a good time. Lots of women say that they love sex even during those times when they don't have an orgasm. Here's some wisdom from the sex clinic where I used to work: *We are all responsible for our own orgasms.*

If your partner does have problems with orgasms, try not to stress too much about it. It's not your fault, and it's not your problem. Don't make her feel uncomfortable about it either. Sometimes a woman needs time to get more comfortable in the sexual relationship before she is able to have orgasms with a partner.

Final note: Older women are usually more orgasmic than younger women. If being with a highly orgasmic woman is important to you, you might want to think in terms of someone who is a little bit older. (And I swear I didn't just put that in as a ploy to get a date.)

chapter eight

PUMP UP YOUR PASSION

Melinda and Bob, who are in their early thirties, have been together for five years. They think they have a good relationship with one major exception: They have so little sex that they both consider it pathetic. This wasn't the case when they first met. Then sex was the most important thing in their relationship. The first weekend they spent together, they had sex so many times, neither thought they would be able to make it to work on Monday morning. They felt as though they were glued together by the sweat on their bodies. Currently, they are having sex once every four to six weeks. Most of the time these days, one or both of them feel as though it is just too much trouble; Melinda would rather watch movies on HBO than have sex; Bob feels the same way about hockey playoffs. They are still young. Melinda is very sexy and appealing; the women in Bob's office describe him as "hot." What's going on with this couple? What can they do about it?

When a couple first hooks up, so to speak, chances are that they are having sex all the time. Every day is not uncommon. Some couples have sex twice a day, or more. As the relationship continues, the couple starts having sex with less frequency; the number of times the couple has sex per week or month may diminish even more and more. This is the norm. But what about when sex diminishes to once a month or less? And what about those healthy singles who rarely want sex? What's going on?

Several studies indicate that a lack of desire is a woman's most common sexual problem. For a long time, it was assumed that few men had the same complaint. The woman was always the one with "the headache." These days, however, modern society makes so many demands on all of us. Go here; go there; do this; do that. Couples with children are overwhelmingly busy and exhausted. Even single people say they don't always have the time. The end result is that even the most sexually inspired men and women are having days and nights when they are lacking in the desire department and feel as though they are not in the mood for sex.

WHAT WE MEAN WHEN WE TALK ABOUT DESIRE

When I first started attending a community college, I was twenty-four, which was a little older than the rest of the students. I had a class I really loved, American history. It was taught by one of the sexiest guys I had ever seen. He was smart; he was distinguished; and he had a voice that made me want to stop whatever I was doing to try to take him home. I couldn't wait to go to class and listen to him lecture. I still remember one lecture he gave about the Salem witch trials. Hey, you never know what's going to turn a woman on. Besides I'm sure I wasn't the only woman in the class who was quivering on the end of her seat.

There was another teacher at the school who wasn't much older than I was, and sometimes he and I would talk together. He knew that I was studying to be a sex therapist, which he found interesting because he liked to talk about sex. One day when I ran into him, he looked really upset and told me he was down in the dumps.

"What's wrong?" I asked him.

"Oh, I just don't feel the same way about sex that I used to," he told me.

He began to describe in great detail how he was accustomed to experiencing high levels of sexual desire and passion, but lately nothing and no one had the power to turn him on. Finally, he said, "I mean, when's the last time you met somebody you were really horny for. I mean do you know anybody who you find so attractive that just thinking about him makes you want to cream your jeans?"

Without thinking about it, I blurted out the name of my history professor, and the two of us started laughing.

The point of this story is that his graphic description of what it means to be totally excited about another person is probably as good a description of the feeling of passion or sexual desire as any. But I certainly don't always feel that kind of immediate desire; none of us do. Who can regularly feel that much intensity or excitement? So does that mean we should give up on sex? Of course not. We need to remember that there are many levels and layers of desire, all of which can be explored. We need to remember that sex is part of what makes life so much fun; sometimes we need to learn to find ways to bring our desire and our passion to the forefront.

FREUD CALLED IT LIBIDO

When I was in graduate school, I took a seminar that I often remember. One of my fellow students was a cute guy (let's call him Leonard) who didn't know he was a cute guy. Leonard had a presentation that was sort of classic nerd. I don't remember if he had a pocket protector or if his glasses were really taped together, but you know the type of guy I mean. Leonard was assigned a project for our seminar: He was supposed to do a presentation on attraction and love. When the time came round for him to speak, he started this incredibly boring presentation. Finally, the professor said something like, "Okay, Leonard, that's enough. I can't take any more. Why don't we just start a discussion by going round the table and each of us try to give our own definition of love? How do you know when you're in love with somebody? Barbara, you start." I said, "It's somebody who really gets your juices flowing." Everyone but Leonard cracked up. In fact, Leonard said, "What does that mean?" Of course, everybody laughed even more. It was pretty good-natured laughter because our class was like a slightly dysfunctional family in which we all tolerated each other's foibles, but it immediately became clear to me that my definition of erotic love/sexual desire clearly relied heavily on a physiological component. Now, that's not true for everybody, and it may not be true for you or your partner. In fact it may not be true for me anymore. (No, I take that back. It's still true.)

Freud receives credit for making sex and desire something that Western civilization could talk about in classrooms as well as bedrooms. He wrote a fair amount about desire, as did Havelock Ellis, Richard von Krafft-Ebing, Charles Darwin, and other important thinkers from the late 1800s and early 1900s. When Freud talked about desire, he called it libido. Some writers and psychologists still do, although others focus more on words like attraction and love.

It's interesting to note that for the most part, Masters and Johnson ignored desire, although all previous theoretical writers had indicated that it was probably the most important variable in whether two people ended up having sex with each other. Remember that Masters and Johnson were scientists interested in being able to precisely measure and define aspects of sexuality. Ways of measuring desire were and are elusive; Masters and Johnson preferred to focus on verifiable data.

In the 1970s, the well-known sex researcher and therapist Helen Singer Kaplan added a desire phase to Masters and Johnson's *sexual response cycle* of excitement, plateau, orgasm, and resolution. Kaplan's very important insight was that sexual behavior begins in the mind long before you get to the bedroom and any sexual activity actually starts. Other social psychologists of the time also started to study the relationship between sexual desire and romantic love. By the 1980s, the concept of desire had become more important. In fact, sex therapists began to see so many patients complaining about inhibited sexual desire that it appeared to be a virtual epidemic. This, even though nobody had yet been able to adequately describe or measure it.

Measuring sexual desire continues to be a huge problem. Some researchers have tried to measure desire indirectly through the measurement of vaginal or penile blood flow. But these are inaccurate because they are actually measures of arousal, not desire. Nonetheless, some people make the assumption that if you become aroused, you must desire sex. This connection is not necessarily true.

Sexual desire has also sometimes been confused with sexual satisfaction, which, when you think about it, is actually its conceptual
opposite. Desire is unfulfilled anticipation; satisfaction is when you
get what you want. There are also two other questionnaire measures
of sexual desire of which I'm aware. Both of these confuse sex drive
and sexual desire. Sex drive, which is testosterone-based, is an inter-
nally induced body and mental state. Sexual desire is connected to
an external object; it is fueled by wanting to have sex with a particular person.

Since desire implies a distance or separation between the person
and the valued object, another thing to keep in mind when we talk
about sex is the element of longing. Sexual desire is a motivational
force that is both intra-individual (located within the person) and
interpersonal, since desire is presumed to be directed at some qualities of the partner. Measures of sexual desire typically fail to distin-
guish between desire for kinky sex and desire for interpersonal sex.
Practitioners of sadomasochism, for example, consistently report
higher levels of sexual desire than people who do not practice SM.
Other questions that purport to measure desire include, "How much
sexual desire do you think you have compared to other people of
your same age and sex?" and "How long could you comfortably go
without sex?"

The measures of sexual desire also confuse frequency and intensity
of sexual desire; for example, a common question is: "How frequently
do you want to have sex?" or "How often do you think about sex or
think about wanting sex?" No one has really studied the various levels
of desire intensity. The closest thing to the most intense levels of
desire is probably that state of being temporarily obsessed with someone and thinking about having sex with that person 85 to 95 percent
of your waking hours. (Tell me about it.)

One of the newer theories about love and sexual desire belongs to

Helen Fisher, a research professor in the Department of Anthropology at Rutgers University. She thinks that romantic or passionate love is a basic human drive and that reproduction is controlled by three different sets of hormones. Testosterone causes our sex drive and makes us want to have sex. Dopamine, a neurotransmitter in the brain, causes us to focus our desire for sex on a specific person; two hormones secreted by the pituitary gland (oxytocin for women and vasopressin for men) stimulate a climate of attachment and intimacy which help create a good environment for child rearing.

In my view, sexual desire has six components:

1. *The physical.* This is the testosterone-based drive that correlates with sexual appetite and plain old-fashioned lust. This physical drive is necessary but in and of itself, it is not sufficient to explain the totality of sexual desire.

2. *Fantasy.* How old were you when you first started daydreaming and having sexual thoughts associated with feelings? We probably start thinking about sexual feelings before we even know what sex is.

3. *Anticipation.* Which comes first, motivation or longing? Whichever, at least part of the fun of sex is derived from the energy and interest connected to the wish to have sex.

4. *Love.* Intense feelings of erotic and romantic passion associated with a specific person will inspire just about anybody to think about sex.

5. *Attachment.* Feelings of fondness and friendship can be an important part of what attracts us to a person. These feelings can grow and change shape.

6. *Becoming proactive.* Taking action and pursuing the object of your desire.

Many people think that the path from hormonal urge to completion of the sexual act is a straight line that should be followed in order. It's not. The importance of the above list is that it shows that if you want to increase desire, you can start at any point and move in any direction. Change one aspect of it, and it will change the whole thing.

Looking at sex in this fashion opens you up to seeing new possibilities and ways of increasing desire and sexual frequency.

DON'T IGNORE LOW DESIRE

Since *impaired desire* is the number-one presenting complaint of people visiting sex therapists, I think it's important that we all think about what that means. By now, I'm sure you have figured out that I am very sexually oriented. I like sex. I like thinking about it, and I like doing it. Nonetheless, there have been days (and sometimes even weeks) where sex is the last thing on my mind. Yes, even the sex therapist is sometimes a little low in the desire department.

When that happens to me, I know that I don't want to continue feeling that way. From professional experience, I also know that people who feel as though they are temporarily turned off to sex can sometimes get into a bad rut of ignoring sex and pretending to themselves and others that they can live without it. This is a very unwise approach. For one thing, if you are in a relationship, it's terrible for intimacy. And if you are alone, avoiding sex is one way of making sure that you don't establish any kind of intimate relationships. So, the obvious question is what to do about it?

The first thing to do if you are going through a bout of low desire is try to figure out what's causing it. Just knowing why can help you find a solution. There are many reasons why both men and women might be feeling less than sexually inspired, but there are also specific reasons for each sex. Here are some of the reasons why passion sometimes takes a back seat:

common reasons why women avoid sex

Feeling Unattractive or Fat

If a woman isn't feeling good about any part of her body, she might not be happy about showing it. I've known women who avoided sex because they had pimples on their backside or zits on their face. Concerns about excess poundage will also make many women avoid sex, or at least sex in well-lit rooms.

Anxiety and Fear

Many fears impact on a woman's sexuality. The most common revolve around a fear of pregnancy or a fear of sexual coercion or abuse.

Hormonal Issues

A woman's hormones wax and wane. Pregnancy, nursing, post-partum depression, menstrual cycle, menopause, and birth control pills all make a difference in how much or little desire a woman may feel. Many women say that their desire is greatly influenced by their menstrual cycle.

Emotional History

Some women carry emotional issues stemming from childhood

or earlier sexual relationships. Sometimes these issues show up immediately; other times even the woman herself may not be aware that something is disturbing her. Sometimes sex only becomes a problem in the context of a committed or deeply intimate relationship.

Insecurity

Many women need a very secure environment in which to express their sexuality. They need to feel very comfortable and confident about the relationship they are in; they need to feel safe. They need to feel that their partners encourage as well as understand their deepest sexual desires. Some women repress their sexual passion if they are not feeling secure about the nature of the relationship.

Something Her Partner Is Doing

I once met a woman who said that her spouse insisted on brushing her teeth before sex. It wasn't because he thought she had bad breath; it was because brushing her teeth turned him on. It sounded a little weird, but perfectly harmless to me, and I certainly try not to make judgments on what people find sexy. However, this woman found it a complete turn-off. Trust me, in bedrooms across American, men and women are turning each other off with similar sexual requests. For example, many women have told me that their boyfriends or husbands want them to talk about having sex with other people (they don't want them to do it, just talk about it). Some women enjoy this, but others find it unpleasant. They say it makes them hate sex. Many women say they hate it when their partners do anything that depersonalizes sex.

common reasons why men lose interest in sex

Hormones

Levels of the male hormone testosterone make a direct difference in how interested a man might be in sex.

Emotional Issues

Stress, anxiety, and depression all make a difference in how sexual a guy feels. A man who is having trouble in the workplace, for example, may also be having trouble in the bedroom.

Performance Concerns

Some men worry because they have difficulty getting and maintaining an erection that they feel good about. Men worry that they will have an orgasm too soon or they may feel shy and unsure of their sexual abilities. These worries will take the fun out of sex and can set up a vicious cycle in which a man might begin to avoid sex.

Something About His Partner

Men can turn off sex because they have turned off on their primary partners. Perhaps she has gained too much weight or she begins to smell exactly like the chocolate cake or tuna fish casserole she ate *after* dinner—and this is true every night! Perhaps she has habits that he can't stand. Perhaps she spends hours on the phone with her mother—and this is also true every night! These habits or behaviors can put a huge damper on a man's sexual desire.

common reasons why both men and women lose interest in sex

Health Issues

Your health impacts on your sexuality. Something as simple as sleep deprivation will reduce your sexual drive. So will thyroid levels as well as other medical conditions. When you are in pain or don't feel well, sex as a concept can become a low priority.

Conflict About the Relationship

Are you confused about whether or not you want a specific relationship to continue? Both men and women cite this as a reason for avoiding sex.

Relationship Problems

Think about all the things that can threaten a relationship. Think about loss of trust and arguments about money and broken promises. Think about infidelity. Think about inappropriate jealousy and possessiveness. Think about anger. Do you feel like having sex with someone at whom you feel angry? Do you feel like having sex with someone with whom you just had a twenty-minute argument over whether or not to turn on the air-conditioning? Think about disrespect and the absence of affection and support. All of these things (and more) can put a major damper on any sexual feelings one might have.

Boredom

You think it can never happen to you, but then it does. You love your partner, but even so, you have settled into less than satisfying sexual rut. Sex is so dull that you both decide that it is easier and more fulfilling to masturbate.

Fear of Sexually Transmitted Diseases

These days, this is not an unusual fear and with good reason. Both men and women worry about the various serious diseases that can be spread through sexual contact.

You Have a Companionate Relationship

What, you ask, is a companionate relationship? It's one in which the partners are close intimate friends who love each other and want to stay together, but who have lost interest in sex. This may sound strange, but there are many relationships like this. I've had men and women tell me that they love their partners and that they are deeply affectionate with each other (they may even sleep spooned around each other), but sex has become a non-issue and a non-event. Often, one or both partners in such relationships make a distinction between sex and affection.

A Cold, Disinterested, or Inattentive Partner

Some people complain that the primary thing wrong with their sex drive is a partner who is lacking in passion. "He's a cold fish!" "I think she is frigid!" These men and women say that their partners appear so disinterested that it hardly seems worth going through the motions to have sex. I once talked to a man who said his wife reached new heights of multitasking. He was doing oral sex on her when she reached over casually to the bedside table, picked up an emery board, and began working on a hangnail. Matching this story is a woman who said that her husband wanted her to do oral sex on the couch while he was watching Sunday night football and eating chips. It was his perfect fantasy come true. It became her nightmare.

A Controlling Partner

Go here; do that! Say this; say that! Lift that leg; raise that hip! Harder! Softer! More pressure! Can't you ever do it right? Some men and women can't stop giving instructions and directions. They want what they want when they want it and how they want it. This isn't about passion or desire; it's about control. Almost inevitably, the partners of these control freaks turn off to sex.

Limited Opportunities for Sex

Babies, small children, teenagers, another resident relative or guest—all of these can create obstacles to a joyous sex life. So can disparate work schedules and sleep patterns.

A Partner with Different Sexual Needs

Greg wants sex three times a week; his girlfriend, Gwyneth, thinks three times a month is about right. Viola expected that when she got married, she'd be having sex every night as well as on Sunday morning. Her husband's response: "Is she out of her mind?" Probably nothing has more effect on someone's desire than being with a partner whose sexual needs are totally out of synch with your own.

Medical Treatments Including Prescription Drugs

This is a *major* issue these days with so many people on antidepressants or other medications that effect sexuality. Birth control pills can impact on sexuality, for example. So can high blood pressure medication and tranquillizers. Many of the drugs prescribed for depression—SSRIs, monoamine oxidase inhibitors (MAOIs), and tricyclics—are frequently implicated in conditions such as erectile dysfunction or orgasm impairment. That means that a man could first have trouble getting an erection, and once he does he might have an equally difficult time having an orgasm. A wide variety of drugs can impact on your sexuality. I recently talked to a man who said that he had hurt his shoulder in a skiing accident so he was taking a commonly prescribed pain medication. As far as he was concerned, the medication dulled a lot more than the pain. These issues with medication affect both men and women.

CONSULTING THE DOCTOR

If you have lost interest in sex, or if you think your ability to have sex is impaired, the first thing on your agenda should be a visit to your doctor's office. Don't put off making an appointment! Get a complete physical and discuss your situation. Make sure you are seeing a doctor who takes your complaints seriously and does the necessary tests. Don't forget to ask him to check your hormone and thyroid levels.

If your sexual issues are connected to a specific medication that has been prescribed, ask if there are similar medications available without these side effects. If you cannot switch your medication (an effective antidepressant, for example), ask your doctor if he has any other suggestions. If you're a man who is having difficulty getting or maintaining an erection, talk to the doctor about drugs such as Viagra, Levitra, or Cialis. These will often compensate for difficulties caused by many prescription medications, including antidepressants.

Something to keep in mind: If your doctor prescribes any new medication, ask him/her about the side effects, including those that are sexual. As ludicrous as it may seem, there are still some doctors who fail to inform their patients. If you can, search the internet and read all the small print.

DRUGS TO IMPROVE
ERECTILE FUNCTION

Scott, age thirty-five, is one of millions of men who have experienced a serious depression. In Scott's case, his depression was at least in part connected to a very stressful and demanding job that he hated, but couldn't really afford to leave. Eventually, his despair over his work situation spilled over into his home life, making him moody and short-tempered. His wife begged him to see a psychiatrist, which Scott finally did. The psychiatrist prescribed an antidepressant and within a couple of months, Scott was beginning to feel better, with one major complication. He couldn't get an erection! Before the medication, Scott was so depressed that he wasn't even thinking about sex, but as his depression lifted, Scott found himself in real conflict. He didn't want to give up the relief that he experienced from the antidepressant, but he also didn't want to live without sex. And he didn't think the situation was making his wife any too happy either.

At forty-nine, Rob thought he was too young to get prostate cancer, but he was wrong. Rob was very fortunate; the disease was caught early, and after treatment, he was assured that the likelihood of it returning was minimal. Although the treatment was a success, it left Rob with a disturbing problem: he couldn't get an erection.

Thomas and his wife—both in their early sixties—had always had a highly charged and pleasurable sex life. He and his wife always thought that their sexual connection was one of the strongest ingredients in their marriage. Then, about a year ago, Thomas noticed that it was becoming more and more difficult to get and maintain and erection. He felt like having sex, but his penis wasn't cooperating.

Even when his penis became erect, it wouldn't stay that way. A larger problem was that both he and his wife had become so discouraged over what was happening that they had stopped trying. Even the idea of sex was becoming frustrating and disturbing. Thomas was beginning to feel old, while his wife was becoming insecure and beginning to wonder if Thomas would have this problem with a younger woman.

Scott, Rob, and Thomas are like millions of other men who go through bouts of erectile dysfunction, but unlike men a few years back, they are very fortunate because there is a possible remedy for their situation, prescription drugs that deal with erectile dysfunction. The first drug on the market was Viagra. Now it has been joined by Cialis and Levitra, and there may be others in the pipeline. The primary difference among the three drugs is how long they remain effective after ingestion. Which drug you take is something for you to discuss with your doctor and your partner. The important thing to know is that there is something that you can do.

There are many reasons for erectile dysfunction ranging from anxiety and stress to diabetes and cardiovascular problems. The good news is that there is now an effective way to address so many cases of erectile dysfunction. One of the main controversies about "erection drugs" is whether you should take them if you technically don't need them. Will any of these drugs turn you into a super stud if your erection is already pretty good? Probably not. But some younger men who have taken erection drugs experimentally or recreationally have noticed that when they take these pills, their erection gets harder and if they have sex once and want to do it again, that second erection comes with greater ease and speed.

If there are no side effects and it doesn't hurt you, is there a downside to taking erection drugs when you don't need them? From my point of view, the answer to that question is, yes. It is possible, for example, to develop such a psychological dependency on erection drugs that you become anxious at the thought of having sex without them.

Another problem is that if you take a pill every time you have sex, even if you don't really need it, sooner or later you're going to have an episode where you think the drug isn't working as well. Either you don't get an erection or the erection you get isn't as hard as it usually is. You may think to yourself, "Oh, this Viagra isn't working." What has probably happened is that you've gotten lazy and relied on the Viagra and lost touch with what you are feeling. Then you take a larger dose the next time and pretty soon you're up to the maximum dose. I've seen this happen. The way to avoid it is to make sure that you aren't neglecting the intimate and sensual aspects of your sexual relationship, the activities that help you get aroused. Because the erection drugs can help you get a strong erection perhaps more quickly, some guys go straight for intercourse and neglect foreplay. Don't fall into this trap. Even if you are using an erection drug like Viagra, start with the lower dose and see if spending a little more time on arousal techniques doesn't give you the same results.

The literature from the manufacturers of all three drugs reminds consumers that these drugs alone will not make you feel desire. However, many men report that they have received an enormous boost in confidence from knowing that their penis is getting a boost from the drug. With this reduced anxiety and newfound confidence, they say that they are able to be more in touch with their desire. The sex lives of many, many men and their partners has improved dramatically from drugs such as Viagra. I think this is a great thing. Remember though, that even with the drugs, you have to feel like having sex in order for them to work.

WAYS TO INCREASE DESIRE

Despite all the negative news about the epidemic of low sexual desire (and all the things that cause low desire) there are many, many ways that have been reliably shown to increase sexual desire. Let's go through some of them.

improve your diet

If you feel overweight, try to lose a few of those extra pounds and see if that doesn't boost your libido as well as your sense of confidence. Cut down on sugar and fat. A healthy diet may be just the boost your sexual energy needs.

exercise regularly

Any form of physical exercise can and probably will increase your sexual desire because it increases dopamine, the brain chemical associated with feelings of passionate love. The best kinds of exercise to increase dopamine are vigorous forms like running, cycling, and swimming. I've found that yoga, Pilates, and floor aerobics work too, not just because they stimulate dopamine, but because the positions often result in unintentional stimulation of the genitals. I'm sure I'm not the only woman who has had an unexpected orgasm in aerobics class. In general, any kind of exercise with pelvic movements is good.

experiment more

Start doing things differently. New places and behavior can add sparks to your sexual relationship. Break your routine and plan a romantic weekend vacation with your sweetie. Even at home, look for some new and novel things to do together. Go dancing, visit amusement parks, or find a sport you can enjoy together. Hey, here's an idea: watch racy movies and start fondling her in the dark during the exciting parts. Start thinking about sex while you are together at the beach, park, or supermarket. Learn to play with your partner and the idea of sex in a new way. When you are shopping for food, for example, buy a can of instant whipped cream and tell her that you're going to write your name across her body and lick it off. Do anything that gets your heart rate up in a sexy way.

improve your fantasy life

People with inhibited sexual desire (ISD) report that they fantasize less often than people who are sexually satisfied. There are other studies that show that frequency of fantasy is correlated with an increase in sexual drive. In fact, a lack of sexual fantasies is one of the two major criteria for ISD (also called hypoactive sexual desire disorder).

Many researchers have attempted to measure frequency of sexual thoughts, daydreams, or fantasies. How they typically do this is to ask their subjects to wear a beeper that goes off at random times during the day. The subjects are instructed that every time their beeper goes off, they are to write down what they are thinking in a journal. Obviously, the researchers don't tell people that they are looking for sexual thoughts or else every time the beeper goes off, everyone would automatically think about sex. One finding from studies using this technique is that men have many more sexual thoughts on a daily basis than women do. People fantasize for many reasons: some fantasize for escapism; others use fantasy to increase arousal during sexual activities. It's interesting to note that men and women typically don't fantasize because they are not getting enough sex. In fact, for women it's the opposite: Women who report high sexual desire as well as a high level of sexual activity and orgasmic ability tend to fantasize more.

It's also interesting to note that when androgens (male hormones) are administered, people report an increase in sexual fantasies. If you feel sluggish in the desire department, I think it's worth your while to put in some time on your fantasy life.

Try using the beeper technique in reverse. Program a beeper or an alarm clock to go off at various intervals during the day. Whenever it happens, think about sex on purpose. Thinking about sex should make you want sex. Try it. See what happens.

If you have no good working sexual fantasies, use reading material or photographs to get you started. Fantasize about an unusual or novel sexual encounter with your current partner. Picture her wearing clothing that you like. Imagine oral sex and exciting new positions. Don't go straight into the genital connection, but instead learn to fantasize the way a woman does. Fantasize an entire romantic encounter from start to finish and do this without masturbating. To boost the novelty factor, think about sex with an attractive stranger you see during the day. If you are in a committed monogamous relationship, you don't have to act on any of these fantasies, but you can use them to get you started.

watch "just enough" porn

What is "just enough" porn? Just enough porn is enough to get you excited, but not so much that you become addicted. My attitude about pornography is a bit conflicted: I can think of several ways that it can help you become more sexual. For example, watching porn will:

- Increase sexual desire, at least temporarily
- Boost the number of times you want to have sex, again temporarily
- Teach you some new sexual behaviors and positions which you can incorporate in your own lovemaking
- Give you permission and show you how to be more sexual in your own life

I can also think of ways in which watching pornography may not help your love life. For example:

- Pornography can desensitize you to the dozens of small wonderful sexual intimacies that can happen between two people.
- You can reach the point where you view so much porn that you need more and more stimulation to turn you on. For example, unless there are two women with incredible bodies have sex with several incredibly over-endowed men, while using dozens of interesting sex toys, it becomes boring and ho-hum.

- Watch too much porn, and you may be come dissatisfied with your own body as well as your partner's body.

- You can also become dissatisfied with what you and your partner do together because you compare it unfavorably with what is happening on screen.

My bottom-line feeling is that a little bit of pornography can stimulate your sexual desire, but too much of it, and it runs the risk of becoming an obsession. Know yourself and try to avoid going overboard.

let go of the idea that sex has to be spontaneous

Our culture values spontaneous sex. We want to believe that the best way to have sex is when desire sweeps over us and we can't stop ourselves. Dream on! I mean, how often does that really happen? In fact, planned sex contributes more to sexual desire than spontaneous sex does because when you plan it, then you get to think about it and look forward to it and that increases desire. Trust me, I've been having planned versus spontaneous sex for years and this approach works. If you start to feel your desire burning out, lay off the sex for a few days and start fantasizing and planning when you will have it next.

have sex even when you don't feel like it

This may be the single best piece of advice I can give to anyone who complains of low sexual desire. Having sex can boost your sexual desire. As Rabelais said, "The appetite grows with eating." I'm not talking about having sex if you find sex repellant; that's a whole other problem. I'm talking about normal circumstances where sex sounds like an okay idea, but you're just not super-horny and you're not sure if you would rather have sex or raid the refrigerator.

Many people think you should have desire before you have arousal, but often it's the other way around. Arousal can cause desire in much the same way that desire causes arousal. They have a reciprocal relationship. It's like eating. You get satisfied after you eat, but eating a lot of great food develops your palate so you want more fine food. Exercising makes you want to exercise more. Drinking good wine make you want to drink more good wine. It works for sex, too.

I always encourage people who with low desire not to retreat from sex, but instead to start being sensual. Start fooling around with each other's bodies in an intimate, nonthreatening manner and see what happens. I will include some suggestions for sexual exercises that will stimulate passion. When we put off or avoid sex, we can sometimes allow our bodies to become turned off. I know that they can be turned on again, and that's what we need to work at. We can't always assume that our hormones and genitals don't need some help and encouragement. Desire has emotional as well as physical components; like everything else, desire and passion need nourishment and care.

The fact is that you don't need perfect or ideal conditions in order to get aroused and have sex. All you basically need is a bed and a couple of bodies. That's it. It's simple: The more sex you have, the more sex you will want, up to a point. Everybody's point is different; it's up to you to find yours!

chapter nine

MAKING HER WANT YOU!

As far as sex and desire are concerned, don't assume that women respond to the same things you do or in the same way—they don't. Men who are described as great lovers have typically taken the time to recognize some of the differences between men and women. I don't want you to feel pressured by this, but it's definitely worth expending some mental energy trying to understand and get a handle on what makes women tick sexually. Doing this should improve your sex life as well as your relationships with women.

The experts still agree: Men's sex drive appears to be much more controlled by nature and women's much more by culture. This has been said by many people in many different ways, but some guys resist hearing this so we're going to say it again. Women are significantly more aware of context, situation, and environment. (That's why she likes candles in the room, while you could care less.)

There have been surveys that say that the male motivation for having sex is primarily sexual release; the primary female motivation, on the other hand, is a feeling that she is in love. For women, romantic love and sexual desire tend to become intertwined and interdependent. From the female point of view, sexual desire is more likely to be connected to a particular person. As I've said before, when she thinks about having sex, she doesn't think about having sex with the body she has seen in a magazine, she thinks about having sex with *you*.

Women in general tend to be more in touch with all the various levels and subtleties of what they are feeling. For example, when men are going through a bout of low desire exacerbated by emotional stress, typically they are either unaware of what is causing it, or won't admit what's causing it. I remember talking once to a man both of whose parents had recently died. For reasons he couldn't "understand," he hadn't felt like having sex since these deaths. He simply couldn't acknowledge that there might be a connection between the personal loss he had suffered and his absence of desire.

A woman is usually quite different. If she is experiencing low desire, she may obsess about what is causing it to the point where she could overlook an attractive potential partner who is staring her in the face. Also keep in mind that women have more potential sexual turn-offs than you do. A woman's drive can quickly be short-circuited by the wrong words or anything that changes the mood. In other words, she can appear to be completely up for sex, but if something distracts her or gets her attention, she can quickly switch to something else.

UNDERSTANDING WOMEN'S SEXUAL GOALS

It's a cliché, but it's true: for women, sex is more about intimacy and emotions. Sometimes I conduct surveys that deal with this question in my classroom. I'm always curious to see whether things have changed for new groups of students. They haven't, so far. Year after year, I get the same results. This is too bad for young women because they are at the height of their testosterone production. On the other hand, even if women fail to be responsive to their hormone production, they seem to have a better grasp of the psychological components of sexual attraction, no matter what their age. In fact, on surveys, many men admit that they don't have a clue about why a partner might or might not desire them.

As a lover, what you always need to remember is that while men are likely to define sex in terms of purely sexual goals, women place it in the bigger context of interpersonal goals. In other words, a man might think, "I want to have sex with Ginger because she is a hottie." A woman, on the other hand, is likely to say, "I want to have sex with Robert because I am in love with him and want to spend the rest of my life with him, and I know he will be a great dad, and I loved the look of surprise in his eyes on Christmas morning when he unwrapped the new CD player I gave him."

Men are consistently more responsive to the purely physical while a woman's sexual desire is strongly influenced by whether or not she feels her intellectual and spiritual needs are being met. This means that a man who wants to make a good impression on a woman he has just started dating can increase her sexual desire for him with the right words and gestures. Every man needs to know and believe this as it is the main reason why some men seem to be able to get all the desirable women. These men know what to say and do, and they know when to say it and do it!

Now, I am not suggesting that you learn to manipulate women by telling them what you think they want to hear. I am suggesting that you get a deeper understanding of what the woman in your life responds to so that you can both have more exciting and more sensual lovemaking.

A friend of mine used to do this monologue where he would compare male and female fantasies. He'd describe the female fantasy first, and he would stretch out this fantasy, which was a very elaborate and detailed story, filled with romantic dinners, sunset walks along the beach, rising music, and the sound of waves. It would be all hearts, flowers, romance, and sensuality. Then he'd do the male fantasy, and the whole thing was reduced to one sentence, "And then I came on her face." Obviously, this is not a female fantasy.

This anecdote reminds me of the mountain of research that shows that men consistently prefer visual stimulation, such as porn-like still pictures and videos, whereas women are more attuned to erotic literature and the written word. By the way, one of the primary reasons women tend not to like the typical male-targeted sex videos is that they prefer something with a narrative structure.

TURNING ON HER PASSION

With a bit of preparation and understanding of the female psyche, you can absolutely help a woman get more excited and encourage her to want sex more often. It always amuses me that people will go to all kinds of trouble to prepare a special meal or party and make everything perfect—the food, the guest list, the décor. But they won't do the same thing to set the stage for a sexual situation. An exception to this was Giovanni Casanova, the man known as the great lover. When he wanted to seduce a woman, he would plan the perfect setting days in advance. He would think about the right music, the perfect food, the ideal wine. If you want to increase a woman's desire, think about female psychology and take some tips from Casanova. Here's how:

find out what turns her on

The first step in being a great lover is to become more sensitive to what the woman you're with finds stimulating, sexy, and erotic. The second step is incorporating her turn-ons in your lovemaking. Hey, *Titanic* may not be your favorite movie, but if watching it with you makes her horny, go for it! Many women become totally responsive while watching movies sitting on the couch or lying in bed with their partners. They like holding hands; they like putting their feet in their partner's lap and having them massaged. They like feeling your body next to theirs for the hour and half or so it takes to watch a movie. This can be a terrific turn-on, particularly if it's the right movie. Find out your partner's preferences in romantic movies and books. The more informed you are about this, the better.

don't forget about the music

Music is a well-documented aphrodisiac. Dancing or listening to fast, pounding music increases your heart rate; sometimes the bass is so strong that you can feel the beat all the way down to your genitals. The typical woman also has a powerful nostalgic streak that is triggered by music. The right music makes her feel romantic, and she loves romance. You can use this to increase her sexual desire. Most of us, for example, grew up with a musical soundtrack in our lives when we were first falling in love. These were the songs we heard when we were driving in cars as teenagers or in our early twenties. Maybe we heard them on warm summer nights when we were on our way back from the beach. When we play the same songs now, we can almost smell the salt air; maybe we heard them on cold winter nights when we steamed up the car with our kisses. When we hear these songs, we can almost feel the stick shift jammed into our back.

People who grew up in the 1940s still get turned on by music from that era. If you grew up in the 1950s, it was Elvis. If you grew up in the sixties or seventies, it was the Beach Boys or the Rolling Stones. What did your partner listen to when she was growing up? For many women, this is a definite turn-on. In short, find out your partner's taste in music and just hope it's not something you hate. If she doesn't have musical memories that excite her, make some new ones.

How about you? Do you play a musical instrument such as the piano or the guitar? Do you know any love songs? Having a man play a musical instrument for you is a huge turn-on. If you're too self-conscious to do it in person, record yourself on tape or CD and play it for her or give it to her, so she can play it in her car.

make her laugh

Laughter is also a huge aphrodisiac. This comes with one caveat: Crude sexual jokes may be funny, but many, if not most, women find them offensive and gross, at least when they are told by a man they care about. It's one thing to hear some dumb comic tell crude jokes; it's quite another to hear a man with whom you're planning to have sex tell them. Major turn-off. Women find conversational humor more of a turn-on; they like humor that is natural and part of the give and take of a conversation. I also know that women tend to say that self-effacing humor can be sexy. They like guys who aren't afraid to laugh at themselves. A night at the Improv can be great foreplay.

show affection

Over the years, I have talked to many women who have complained that the only time their husbands and boyfriends touch them is when they want sex. They say things like, "He ignores me all the rest of the time and then all of a sudden, he wants sex, and he expects me to feel the same way. Well, I don't. I can't turn on and off like he does."

Keep that in mind and keep the physical connection between you and your partner strong even when sex is nowhere on the horizon. Don't forget about kissing just for the fun of kissing.

show your passion

Passion is probably the number one turn-on for both men and women. Nothing is more exciting than a passionate lover and nothing is more discouraging than a lover who lacks sexual enthusiasm or interest. Let me tell you a little story: About a year ago, my friend Casey started dating Joe, a guy she met through an internet dating service, and at first, she was very attracted to him. He was age-appropriate; they shared lots of similar interests, as well as similar politics; and he seemed sincere and intelligent, as well as cute. They e-mailed each other for a few weeks; then they talked on the phone. For their first date, they met for coffee. On their second date, they went out to dinner. Casey was impressed that Joe didn't try to make any moves on her. It made her feel that he wanted to get to know her better. She liked that.

For their third date, they took a long drive in the country, stopped to eat at a clam shack, and went to a movie. Joe didn't even seem to want to hold Casey's hand during the movie, which seemed odd. On the next date, they went to a concert in the park; they brought a picnic. The picnic was lovely: cold barbecued chicken; juicy, ripe tomatoes; olives; homemade potato salad; and a perfect bottle of chilled chardonnay. Joe didn't ask to kiss Casey good night; he did, however, ask for her potato salad recipe. They made another date—to go to the beach and hang out together on a Saturday afternoon. Casey arrived at Joe's place at noon. They went to visit his cousin who has a house on a beach; they came back to his house and took a walk; they ordered in a pizza and watched a video. At ten P.M., as Casey was about to leave, she couldn't believe that there had been no physical contact. She felt very drawn to the man with whom she had spent the day so she spontaneously reached out to give Joe a hug. He gave her a weak hug back. Through his trousers, Casey could feel an erection. She moved closer. He moved back. What was going on here?

Casey went out with Joe three more times, and they did finally engage in some foreplay. Casey reported back that Joe seemed to have no difficulty in getting an erection, but he seemed to have zero enthusiasm for sex. In the passion department, Joe scored a little bit lower than zilch. No matter how hard she tried to get him to move forward, he never seemed as lusty about her as he had been about her potato salad.

"He's like a dead man as far as I'm concerned," Casey said. "I can't tell what his story is. Either he doesn't like me or he doesn't like sex. If either of these is the reason, this isn't going to work. The next time Joe called, Casey told him that the relationship wasn't working for her, and she also indicated that she got the impression that Joe wasn't that interested in her. He mumbled something about how he could understand what she was saying; he got off the phone, and that was that.

More than six months later, Casey ran into Joe's cousin at a shopping mall. The cousin seemed happy to see her and immediately began talking to her. "I'm so sorry it didn't work out between you and Joe," the cousin said. "Joe is never attracted to anybody, and he said you were the hottest woman he had ever met." Casey said she was shocked to hear this because Joe never seemed that "into" her.

"That's strange," the cousin told her. "Joe's ex-wife said almost exactly the same thing."

The point of this story is that women want to know that you want them sexually. Before you have sex, they want to feel your desire. When you are having sex, they want to feel that you are excited and aroused. They want to share in that excitement. How can you convey that passion? Here are some suggestions:

- Gaze deeply into her eyes and hold the gaze. Then smile in a way that lets her know that you find her desirable. Do this when other people are around, and your attraction for each other will be your little secret.

- Let your hands graze over parts of her body that are not normally thought of as sexual—her shoulders, her elbows, her hair.

- Hold her hand when you cross the street.

- When you are at the movies, hold her hand and stroke her arm.
- Kiss her neck.
- Kiss the inside of her elbow.
- If you are at the beach, kiss the tops of her knees when you get up off the blanket.
- If you combine any of the above gestures with a little bit of eye-gazing, it will go a long way. Know your partner and don't be afraid to experiment with the types of things that will demonstrate your passion for her.

show her that you are interested in knowing more about her

When a woman likes a guy, she wants to know everything about him, and she wants him to know more about her. That's because she wants to deepen and intensify both the spiritual and the sexual connection. Many, if not all, women feel that when they are able to share their feelings and their experiences, it deepens their sense of trust. This feeling of trust is a very important element in a woman's sexuality.

So, yes, it's a good thing to ask a woman about her sexual responses and her relationship history—if you do it in the right way. But, and this is a *big* but, it's a bad thing to ask a woman about her sexual history in the wrong way. There is a right and a wrong way to ask a woman to confide her feelings about sex. Don't, for example, ask her the details about how she had sex with anybody else. Most women find that creepy. In fact, if you ask her about the details of her sexual history in a way that she finds creepy, it's going to make her completely distrust you. (Another good reason why you don't want to ask her about too many details about past loves is that many men ultimately find it threatening to the relationship, even when it's not.) But you can ask her about general dynamics of past relationships without going into details, and you can ask her about what kind of situations and environments she finds sexually stimulating in general.

You can probably safely ask her about her first crush, which usually happened somewhere between the ages of six and twelve. Ask her about situations that turned her on in the distant past, like when she was still a teenager. If she talks mostly about the emotions involved, don't immediately switch to her sexual reactions and thoughts. Again, she will find that creepy. If she does give you information about her sexual history, don't be threatened by what she tells you. Ask her about the times in her life when she felt the most sexual, sensual, and excited. The information you find out will far outweigh your need to be jealous. I have an illustration of this from my own life. Years ago, I had a crush on a Catholic priest. It was so intense that for years, the sight of a clerical collar turned me on. I've gotten over this, which is probably a good thing, considering my line of work. But I did tell a boyfriend of mine about this, and the next time he came over he was wearing a black outfit with a clerical collar that he had ordered online. (P.S. It worked.)

Another word of warning here: Several women in my classes said that they didn't always like telling men what they wanted sexually. The reason: Some guys have a tendency to get fixated on that one thing, becoming what these women described as "one-trick ponies."

use words to make her feel more sensual

"How do I love thee, let me count the ways."

Poet Elizabeth Barrett Browning used these words to tell her husband Robert Browning how much she cared. For many people, sex is a form of poetry. The best lovers know how to share their feeling with the words they use; they know that words are an aphrodisiac.

It's true that we show our passion with our bodies, but we can also convey passion and sexuality with our words. Words are an important part of the sexual experience. They can make your lover feel as though she is melting and lead to less inhibited and more responsive lovemaking.

Tell her how much you like her body. Be specific. If you can't find ways to describe the body parts you particularly love, don't worry about it, just say it, "I love your breasts. They're so beautiful," or "Your legs drive me out of my mind." If you want to be more graphic to describe what you are seeing, you can always liken her body to flowers or fruit. "Your legs are like long elegant irises in the spring," or "Your breasts are like perfect peaches." You may feel self-conscious uttering such hokey sentences, but try to find something that seems right to you. When a woman is complimented in this way, she remembers it. A friend of mine said that she fell in love with her husband because he told her that her vagina smelled like fresh vanilla. I remember once meeting a woman who said that her husband of thirty years surprised her one day by telling her that she reminded him of a ripe pear that he couldn't wait to eat. She said that every time she got angry with him, she remembered that sentence and it immediately changed her attitude.

Words are also an essential way to convey what we enjoy. Sharing our pleasure with words is incredibly arousing. Some of these words are loving and caring, but others are just plain sexy. Many men's idea of sexy talk begins and ends with four-letter words. If this is the case with you, there is a lot more you need to know. Here's a rule of thumb: four-letter words are not okay with some women in any situation. A woman is more likely to be okay with this in a sexual context when she really turned on, but even then, the tone of your voice is very important. If you whisper four-letter words in her ear combined with sweet intimate personal phrases, you are going to have much better results than if you spew four-letter words into the air in an impersonal way.

There is an episode of *Sex in the City* that deals with this. In it, one of the female characters, Charlotte, has a lover who spews four-letter words at her just as he is about to have an orgasm. She finds it a total turn-off, and it is quickly apparent that it is just something he does with everyone. In fact, when she asks him about it, he has no memory of what he has said. This also illustrates how distant and remote some men can become during sex.

A woman wants to know that she is the person who is turning her partner on. So if you use four-letter words, keep it personal and affectionate. Walk up to your partner at a party when no one is around and whisper something sexy in her ear, but keep it intimate and specifically directed at her. It's a good idea to combine four-letter words with words of endearment. As in, "You're my sweet sexy sweetie, and as soon as we get home, I want to (choose your phrase)." I don't think I need to tell you that you shouldn't try this approach with a woman you don't really know.

Words will enhance a woman's sexuality if you use them to encourage her to be more open and to explore her sexuality. You can, as I've said before, encourage her to show you how she wants to be touched. You can say things like, I love looking at your (name the specific body part). I love touching your (name the specific body part). Show me how you want me to touch your (name the specific body part).

If you are with her, I'm assuming that you find her desirable. Tell her all the ways that you think that she is sexy, sensual, and desirable. Make her feel what you feel. It doesn't matter what words you use, as long as you convey that message.

When it comes to sharing our sexual feelings with our partners, we're all a little too shy and just about everybody can use some help. It's important to recognize when you are being appropriately and charmingly sexual and when you are being an inappropriate boor. You can tell whether your partner is responding by her body language and the expression on her face. Pay attention. If she seems to be moving away instead of moving toward you, that what you are doing isn't working, and you need to rethink your approach.

show her that you accept her *and* her sexuality

Your words can help her feel that you accept all of her and that you accept and encourage her sexuality. This is a major-league turn-on. Women want to feel safe and accepted. Many women know from firsthand experience that there are men who will turn on a dime and walk away from women who they find "too" sexual. Some men still have that split in their heads about women you love and marry and women you love and have sex with. Make sure you are not one of those men!

Enjoy and encourage your partner's sexuality. Once again, tell her how much you like her body and help her become more comfortable with her imperfections. Help her gain more confidence in how she looks. Encourage her to wear flattering clothing and appealing colors, and go shopping with her at least once and help her pick out something. Most women like it when their partners choose sexy lingerie. Underwear is tricky because of size and comfort issues, but a beautiful camisole or something to sleep in or lounge in is usually appreciated. Choose a fabric that you enjoy touching and that you think will feel good next to her body. Every time she wears it, she'll think of you.

Most important, don't encourage her to be more sexual and then reject her for doing what you requested. I don't want you to think that I rely on TV for all my research, but sometimes a picture is worth a thousand words, as they say. With that in mind I'd like to tell you about yet another episode of *Sex in the City*, which paints a particularly vivid picture of this unfortunate trait. In this episode, Miranda is having sex with somebody who encourages her to "talk dirty" during sex. At first she is grossed out, but eventually she starts to get into this activity. The problem is that once she does, she begins to use words and describe acts that her male partner finds offensive. Many women are naturally insecure about using four-letter words, and they are also aware that it can turn into a relationship deal-breaker if they do it in the wrong way. It's up to you to be both encouraging and accepting of the totality of your partner's sexuality.

don't rush her

Now that I've told you to show your passion, I'm going to tell you not to push or rush sex. Does that seem like too much to ask? I understand why you might feel that way. Last week, I was home watching a competitive diving event. Those divers were amazing. They jumped off the high board backward and forward; they did twists and turns and back flips and somersaults in the air. Amazing. Then, as they hit the water, they glided in. If they splashed, they lost points. Doesn't that seem like too much—to be able to do all those tricks in the air, and then hit the water without splashing?

Making a woman want you can require the same kind of grace. When Olympic-level divers enter the water seamlessly with barely a ripple, it shows the level of their confidence and their control.

Men who are great lovers are able to show their passion without losing their sense of control and confidence. Remember that. You want to show a woman that you want her, but you want to convey an aura that lets her know that you are in control of yourself and the situation. What more can I say? I know it sounds complicated, but it's really not. Show her that you are sexy, but don't make her feel that you are needy or desperate for her. It's not very attractive. At least not until she knows you better. Then sometimes it's a different story.

Remember that romantic love is stimulated by thwarted sexual desire. Sometimes it helps to play a little hard to get. Don't be too easy. It will only make her want you more. Artificial barriers to having sex also increase desire. It's kind of sneaky, but figure out a way to put imaginary obstacles between you without being dishonest and without making her feel that you are avoiding sexual contact. I know this requires some finesse, but once again remember those Olympic divers entering the water without making a splash.

keep sex interesting

When you're in your late teens and twenties, it seems difficult to believe that sex could ever become boring. But then where do all those people come from—the ones complaining to therapists about a boring or nonexistent sex life?

In truth, I don't think that sex ever becomes boring, and I don't think that's what people complain about. What they are usually complaining about are sexual relationships and intimate interactions that have become boring. Masturbation, for example, rarely becomes boring. But getting annoyed with a partner who has kept you waiting in the rain can make you bored with that person and bored with anything they do, including sex. The point is that you should always remember that sex happens in the context of a connection between two people.

Here are some suggestions for making sex more interesting.

- Have sex in different locations even within your own house. Have sex in the bedroom, but also have sex in the shower. Have sex in the guest room, but also have sex in the living room.
- Have sex in different positions. Have sex sitting in a chair; have sex standing against a wall; have sex lying on a bed. Be creative and use your imagination. Make love with your clothes on; make love partially clothed; make love when she is wearing your clothes.
- Don't do exactly the same thing every time in exactly the same sequence. Some people get into routines such as, "First, I do oral sex; then she does oral sex; then we have intercourse." Surprise your partner. It's fun!

find some female-friendly porn

Yes, many women will respond to the right kind of soft porn. But, if you hope that the typical woman, who has probably not been exposed to much porn, will become more passionate after watching porn, you have to be sure that it's the right kind of porn that has been introduced in the right way.

I know that most men like porn, and that's nothing to be embarrassed about. I like porn myself, even though I acknowledge that the majority of women might not agree with me. When I was in grad school, one of my fellow students was trying out a questionnaire for her dissertation project on her fellow students. The questionnaire had a range of statements with which you were supposed to agree or disagree. One of the statements was "Pornography is disgusting." Of course I wrote, "Strongly agree—and that's why I like it."

Men and women differ greatly in their reactions to sexually explicit material. This difference goes way beyond the cliché, "Men are more visual." Both men and women get turned on when they see naked bodies. Women lubricate, and men begin to get erect.

The major difference between men and women is that men usually recognize and acknowledge their excitement and arousal, while women usually don't. Many women don't even realize that they are lubricating, or if they do, they may look around to see what is getting them aroused. Then if they don't like what they see, they deny that they are sexually excited. What this means is that a woman can view sexually explicit materials and be physically aroused without experiencing any psychological arousal whatsoever. Even as she is lubricating, she could look at a pornographic video and say, "That's disgusting. I couldn't possibly be getting turned on by that!"

What I'm saying is that even though I like some porn, I don't think that you can assume that porn will automatically turn a woman on in the same way it does you. Also, I don't think your sexual partner is ever going to have the same taste in porn that you do. Having said that, if you want to try watching porn with your partner, I'd suggest that you find films that have more of a story line. Your partner might like some of the older porn movies made back in the seventies. Many of them are funny as well as sexy, and women are often more receptive to the mix of humor and pornography.

share some fantasies

Before you or your partner start sharing all kinds of fantasies, I think it's important that everybody understands that this can be treading in dangerous territory. If either of you have a tendency to jealousy, it can play havoc with your relationship.

Having said that, I do think that fantasies can play an important role in jazzing up your sex life. To keep things less emotionally threatening, however, I like to suggest that couples focus on fantasies that increase their knowledge and awareness of each other and don't add any new and jarring elements. Here are some "safe" fantasies to share with your partner.

- "I like to imagine you going down on me in a restaurant. I can see you down under the table with your fingers creeping up my thigh. . . ."
- "I like to imagine you taking my hand and bringing my fingers to your vagina and showing me how to put them in you just the way you like. . . ."
- "I like to fantasize about the first time we had sex and how hard you were breathing when you were about to have an orgasm. I like imagining that you are asking me to enter you. . . ."

You will note that all of these fantasies involve the *two of you* and no one else. Because of this, they should not be threatening to your relationship. Fantasies that include other partners can introduce elements that might disturb your relationship so be aware of this and act accordingly.

try some new-age sex techniques

Think all that yoga, new-age stuff is wacky? Think again because maybe it can bring your sex life into a whole new zone. There are dozens of ways of encouraging desire that might be called new-age. Some people use dancing as a way of loosening up. Others love to take baths together, complete with candles and luxurious soaps, gels and oils. Still others rely on sun and sand. I have friends who have a summertime ritual: Every Sunday afternoon they go to the beach where they hang out on the sand and swim in the surf. After a couple of hours of this, they go home, take relaxing showers together, put on some mood music, and take a nap. They say the intimacy of sleeping together helps bond them. When they wake up, they have terrific sex. Personally, I might skip the nap and go straight to the sex, but I agree about the beach and sunbathing. I also find it very sexy and sensual.

Anything that loosens up our bodies and increases sexuality and relaxation can be termed "new-age." Keep that in mind as you look for new ways to stimulate desire.

My friend Bettine says that the best lover she ever met was a man named Zack; she met him at a resort where she was vacationing with some friends. Every morning, Bettine would go down by the pool where Zack would inevitably be surrounded by a group of women in towels. Zack, who was a lawyer in his work life, loved to give massages. He was great at it. Giving massages had given Zack exceptionally strong and sensitive hands. Zack never crossed any boundaries during his massages; he was never inappropriate and never acted as though he was aroused, which made women feel comfortable and, here's that word again, "safe." Nonetheless, just about any woman whom Zack massaged also wanted to go to bed with him.

It turned out that Bettine and Zack were neighbors and lived in the same city so they stayed in touch and eventually became lovers. Their relationship didn't last, but Bettine still remembers Zack's hands and his lovemaking. She told me that he was an expert at new-age love making. Frequently, when they had sex, he totally set the scene. He would light candles and put on romantic music. Sometimes they would take a bath or shower together; he always had lovely lotions and creams and they would take turns massaging each other's bodies. By the time they began actual intercourse, Bettine said that she was more aroused than any other time in her life.

Most people agree: *The more emotionally open, receptive, and in the moment you are, the better the sex.* New-age lovemaking techniques can help you and your lover achieve this goal. Some couples, of course, will never learn how to massage each other, but they can still visit a body worker or a spa together and come home to experience sex while their bodies are still relaxed. New-age sexuality is all about attitude; it's about being willing to be open and sensitive; it's about being willing to become more sensual and spiritually connected to your partner. Here are a few techniques to get you started.

Make Eye Contact While You Breathe Together

Making eye contact with your partner increases a sense of intimacy, and breathing is very connected to your sexual energy. The next time you and your partner are having sex, suggest that you try this exercise: Lie down on a comfortable bed or couch and face each other. You can hold each other if you like or you can touch each other. Make eye contact and continue gazing into each other's eyes. As you do this, start breathing slowly through your nostrils and then exhaling through your mouth. In breath through the nose; out breath through the mouth. Continue looking into each other's eyes. Start synchronizing your breathing. Use slow, steady breathing. Feel the breath go down to your genitals. Look into your partner's eyes. Can you begin to see her excitement? Continue breathing this way for several minutes. Incorporate this technique into your lovemaking. As you are having sex, maintain eye contact. Breathe in harmony with each other. As you start having sex, breathe slowly; then as you both become more aroused and excited, breathe more quickly. Most people say that this kind of breathing enhances everything they feel in the genitals. It can also intensify orgasm. Remember that women like to make eye contact. It intensifies the connection between you.

Give Her the World's Greatest Foot Massage

I venture to say that it's a rare woman who doesn't respond to a man who has the sensitivity and skill to massage her feet. If you want, you can do this for a woman on her birthday or some other special event. It's a real treat and very, very sexy. Here's what you'll need:

- A large dishpan that will comfortably accommodate your partner's feet
- Hot water
- Several towels
- A pair of white cotton socks
- Some liquid soap or a package of dry soap flakes
- Vaseline
- A foot scrub. The one I've used is called Pretty Feet. An exfoliant or rough skin remover, this has a grainy texture that

sloughs off the top layers of dry skin. There are other examples of this type of product; look in a drugstore or health food store.

Step #1: Set the stage.

Choose a good place to do this. If you have a secluded deck or backyard, that's terrific. If not, the bedroom is fine. Wear something that you are comfortable about getting wet: a bathing suit or shorts with no shirt or even just a towel are all appropriate. Put on some music that you both like. Tell her that you want to do something special and relaxing.

Step #2: Rinse her feet in warm water.

This will soften the skin and prepare it for the next step.

Step #3: Use the sloughing product (foot scrub) as directed on both of her feet.

The purpose of this is to massage her feet and get rid of the dry skin. This is one time when you can use a much firmer touch on her feet than you usually would for sexual activity.

Step #4: Fill the dishpan with warm water and put the soap in it.

Have her sit in a chair with both her feet in the pan while you gently wash them to get rid of the skin and the sloughing agent from the previous step.

Step #5: Take her feet out of the pan one at a time.

Gently pat them dry. Give at least one of them a gentle kiss. Then, while they are still damp, open the Vaseline. Again, one foot at a time, coat it with Vaseline. Yes, Vaseline, and use a lot of it. I know this may sound weird, but it really works. I hear they do this at some of the most expensive spas (except of course for the kiss), and I can understand why.

Step #6: As soon as you are finished applying the Vaseline, put a sock on each foot.

Tell her to leave the socks on for at least half an hour to absorb the Vaseline. When the socks come off, her feet will be as smooth and soft as baby skin.

and, finally, fall in love

The most common sexual fantasy reported by both men and women is "having sex with someone I'm in love with." Being in love can cause sexual desire and desiring someone sexually can cause you to fall in love with that person. So if you want a woman to feel sexual desire for you, you need to get her to fall in love with you. To make yourself her sex object, make it clear that's how you feel about her. If you think she is beautiful and special, let her know it. If you love talking to her, share that information with her. Treat her like she's the most precious and attractive woman in the world, and you'll get a self-fulfilling prophecy working for you.

appendix

SEXUAL INTELLIGENCE, STDs, AND BIRTH CONTROL

In an ideal Garden of Eden world, there would be no sexually transmitted diseases (STDs); there would be no unwanted pregnancies; and there would be no sexual problems. Unfortunately, we don't live in that kind of world. STDs appear to be running rampant and becoming more exotic every day. We all know that unplanned pregnancies happen to people of every race and economic background.

Men who have the necessary information about these topics appear more confident and sophisticated. They seem to be more in control and grounded in reality. Men who don't have this information can appear naïve and out of touch. Here are some things a man needs to know to help him be in control as well as appear in control. Having a firm grip on this information will help you handle your relationships and sexual health in an informed way.

SEXUALLY TRANSMITTED DISEASES ARE REAL

When I first became sexually active, people weren't all that concerned about STDs. HIV and AIDS were terms nobody had yet heard. Syphilis was erroneously thought of as something that happened to people hundreds of years ago—mostly to men and women who didn't bathe that often, like European artists and nobility of the time; herpes was a non-issue as far as most people were concerned. Every now and then, you would hear of somebody who got gonorrhea, which was uncomfortable but curable, thanks to modern antibiotics.

Wow, times have certainly changed. It is now estimated that one in five sexually active adults has an STD. Every sexually active person should have some understanding of STDs and better ways to prevent them. It's part of being sexually savvy, sophisticated, and aware.

WHAT IS A SEXUALLY TRANSMITTED DISEASE?

STDs are diseases that are transmitted through sexual contact. They can be spread through vaginal, oral, or anal contact.

Some STDs are bacterial; others are viral. There are cures for bacterial STDs, but unless there is a major breakthrough and cure, those that are caused by viruses will be in your body for the remainder of your life.

THE MOST COMMON BACTERIAL STDs

Chlamydia is very common. It is estimated that four million sexually active Americans get chlamydia each year. Do you want to read that number again? Most of these are teenagers or young adults. The primary symptoms of chlamydia are painful urination or a discharge. However, you can have chlamydia and have no symptoms whatsoever. The long-term problems from untreated chlamydia are reproductive. For men, the infection can affect the ability to make viable sperm. Some infections leave men unable to father children. For women also, a chlamydia infection can do serious damage to the reproductive system.

To know for sure whether you have chlamydia, you need to be tested by a doctor. If you discover that you have chlamydia, prompt medical treatment with the appropriate antibiotic is essential and effective.

Gonorrhea is another bacterial infection that can affect anyone who is sexually active. Close to 500,000 new cases are diagnosed each year. If you were to have symptoms from gonorrhea, they would probably include painful urination and a discharge. But again, it is possible to have a full-blown gonorrheal infection and not know it until it is so far advanced that your health and well-being are jeopardized. Ten percent of men with gonorrhea don't have any immediate recognizable symptoms. With women, this percentage is much higher. A few years back, I knew a woman who had gonorrhea and wasn't aware of it until pain and a high fever brought her to an emergency room in the middle of the night. She was fortunate in that a quick-thinking doctor saved her life by ordering an immediate emergency hysterectomy.

The only way to know for sure if you have gonorrhea is to get test-ed. If you have any symptoms—including pain or discharge—get yourself to a doctor immediately. If you suspect that any of your partners could be infected, get tested and seek treatment, which includes the appropriate antibiotic.

<u>Syphilis</u> is not as widespread as chlamydia or gonorrhea. Even so, many thousands of new cases are reported each year in the United States. Syphilis is a peculiar disease in that it goes through several distinct phases. During the primary phase of the disease, there may be one or more painless sores or chancres that appear from three weeks to three months after being infected. These sores, which can appear on the genitals, mouth, or anus, can last several weeks or quickly disappear. During this phase, there may also be swollen glands. The secondary phase of a syphilitic infection usually occurs from three to six weeks after the sore or sores appear. These symp-toms include other kinds of body rashes, sometimes on the palms of the hand or the soles of the feet. Other symptoms include hair loss, fatigue, inexplicable fevers, headaches, and muscle pains. These symptoms typically disappear after this phase is over.

The next phase of syphilis is called the latent phase, during which there are no symptoms. This phase can last for years. The most seri-ous problems associated with syphilis occur if the disease is left untreated until the late or final phase, when syphilis starts attacking the nervous system, heart, or brain. At this stage, there can be severe neurological damage or even death.

I know a couple of people who have been diagnosed with syphilis. The first is an average guy working an average job; he wasn't even particularly sexually active. He was never sure exactly how he got the disease. He had no awareness of any initial sore, but he did remember having a peculiar rash, which he discussed with several friends. He even consulted a doctor about the rash. Unfortunately, the doctor scratched his head and said he didn't have a clue what it was, but come back if it didn't go away. The rash went away (as syphilis rashes do), and my friend forgot all about it. A couple of years later, my friend, who by now had married, and his wife visited a doctor because they were having trouble conceiving. The doctor ran every test in the book on the couple, including a blood test for syphilis. This is a test most doctors don't routinely suggest, and my friend was very lucky. Once the syphilis was diagnosed, it was cured with a course of antibiotics, but it was pure luck that he was diagnosed before it was too late.

The second person was the sixty-plus-year-old mother of a friend who contracted the disease while undergoing surgery and receiving a transfusion. This definitely falls under the you-never-know category, but it reminds us that we need to be very cautious and do what is necessary in terms of testing and protection from STDs.

Urinary tract infections (UTIs) are typically bacterial, but they are not always thought of as STDs. I'm including them because they can spread through sexual contact. They are most often caused because bacteria have somehow spread from the rectum to the penis or vagina. It is then only a short trip up to the bladder and urethra. You don't need an illustration to figure out how they can be transmitted during sexual activities. Women seem to complain of urinary tract infections more often than men. Many of you have heard the term "honeymoon cystitis" to describe the mild infections women can get after having lots and lots of sex with lots and lots of thrusting.

The symptoms of a UTI include pain, frequent urination, or a feeling of needing to urinate even when the bladder is empty.

Sometimes there is blood or pus in the urine, and sometimes there is a fever. Some women say that wearing a diaphragm makes them more prone to UTIs. Other women say that the angle at which a man's penis penetrates during sex can make a difference. Once again, if a woman is treated for a UTI, it is probably a good idea for her partner to visit his physician to see if he should be treated as well, even if he has no symptoms. UTIs can become more serious if they are left untreated. From the male point of view, I have seen literature to indicate that they sometimes contribute to more serious kidney infections, as well as prostatitis.

Many people don't realize that a urinary tract infection can pass back and forth between sexual partners, even though one of them may be symptom-free.

VAGINAL INFECTIONS

Trichomoniasis is often considered a vaginal infection because women are more likely to have distressing symptoms than men. But make no mistake, it is a STD, and it can be transmitted when one partner has it. Women's symptoms include an unpleasant-smelling discharge, itching, frequent urination, and sometimes pain. Many men have no symptoms, but the most common male symptoms are a discharge and a sensation of burning while urinating. The condition is pretty common, up to five million diagnoses a year, but it's easily cured with the right drugs. When a woman visits a doctor and is prescribed drugs for this condition, it's important to treat her partner as well. The most common treatment is metronidazole, also known as flagyl. It's wise not to have sex while being treated for trichomoniasis in order to reduce the possibility of passing it back and forth.

Yeast infections are associated with vaginal infections, but they really can happen to both men and women. Although they can be sexually transmitted, they are also triggered by a wide variety of other reasons including stress and tight clothing, so there is no point in playing any kind of blame game. Yeast infections are associated with anything that changes the acid/alkaline balance in the vagina. Harsh soap, for example, can create problems. Antibacterial soaps kill off friendly as well as nonfriendly bacteria, and they are sometimes implicated in these kinds of infections. Some women complain of yeast infections if they are using a spermicide that includes nonoxynol-9. Taking oral antibiotics can also make people more susceptible to yeast infections. The symptoms include typically include discomfort, itching, or a rash. There are over-the-counter medications for yeast infections, but if they continue you should see a doctor.

COMMON VIRAL INFECTIONS

Since viruses can live in your body for long periods of time without causing symptoms, there is often no way to tell how long the infection has been in your body or how you got it. There are millions of people out there who carry the herpes or human papilloma viruses. They may have never had an outbreak and they may not even be aware that they harbor the virus.

Human papilloma virus (HPV) is the term for the various viruses that cause genital warts, as well as other conditions. These viruses are very common and it's estimated that as many as twenty million men and women are now infected. Many HPV infections are mild and symptom-free; others are more problematic and are directly linked to cancers of the cervix, vulva, and penis. When HPV causes warts, they typically appear in the genital area. In men, they may appear on the penis, but they can also be detected on the scrotum or around the anus. If there are warts associated with HPV, they usually appear within three weeks to six months after exposure. There is no known cure for HPV, although the warts themselves (which may recur) can be removed. As with all STDs, if you think you may have HPV, it is essential that you visit a doctor and inform your partner. In turn, she needs to visit her doctor and find out what she needs to do to protect herself.

Hepatitis B, which is an infection of the liver, is caused by a virus that is easily transmitted. You can get it by sharing saliva—kissing someone or, for that matter, sharing a soda. You can also get it from vaginal, oral, or anal sex. The symptoms of hepatitis B usually develop within two to six weeks after exposure. They might include headaches, fatigue, nausea, vomiting, light-colored stools, dark-colored urine or yellowing of the eyes and skin (known as jaundice).

Most people who contract hepatitis B have a complete recovery. In a small percentage, however, the disease becomes chronic, and can lead to more serious liver problems. The good news about hepatitis B is that it can be prevented by a vaccine.

Genital herpes, unfortunately, is well on its way to becoming the most common STD. It is currently estimated that one in four Americans have been exposed to this virus. Some people with herpes have absolutely no symptoms. Other people have mild symptoms that disappear in a few days; still others have painful or uncomfortable breakouts that recur with some regularity. Recurrences tend to become milder and less frequent with time. The typical symptoms of genital herpes are small sores that resemble blisters in the genital area, often combined with swollen glands. Although there is no cure, there are treatments that speed up the healing process and help reduce recurrences. Some people have outbreaks with some frequency; others may be outbreak-free for years. The first thing to do if you suspect genital herpes is to visit your doctor.

The bottom line is that herpes is a skin disease that millions of people live with. It's certainly not the end of the world. It is possible to have a sexual relationship with somebody with herpes and not contract the disease. People who get herpes tend to become hysterical at their first outbreak. Within a short time, however, they realize that it's very manageable. Your doctor can give you sound advice on how to reduce symptoms and protect yourself and your partner.

Human immunodeficiency virus (HIV) is the most dangerous of all the STDs. Currently, it is the fifth major cause of death for Americans between the ages of twenty-five and forty-four. It has been estimated that there are as many as 40,000 new cases a year in the United States. As yet, there is no cure for HIV.

HIV is found in semen, vaginal secretions, blood, spinal fluid, and breast milk. Urine, saliva, and tears can also contain the virus, but in such small amounts that it is believed that the virus cannot normally spread this way.

Although there may be some flu-like symptoms or a rash or diarrhea initially after being infected with HIV, these usually disappear and there may be no further symptoms for ten or more years. HIV proceeds in stages depending on how compromised your immune system is. As HIV progresses, symptoms include unexplained weight loss, diarrhea, fatigue, unexplained fevers, cough, little or no appetite, night sweats, thrush infections of the tongue or mouth, vaginal yeast infections, and headaches.

The sooner you are treated for HIV, the better the outlook. You can be tested for HIV at most clinics and doctors' offices as well as by the health department. It can take as long as three to six months after exposure for the virus to be detectable in the blood. There are many new treatments for HIV, some of which have been very successful in holding the virus at bay. Since there are no reliable early symptoms of HIV, it's really important for men and women who are sexually active to use condoms faithfully and be tested regularly.

PROTECTING YOURSELF AND YOUR PARTNER

I am the first one to acknowledge that having to think about "safer sex" is really tedious. I don't like it any more than the next person. Nonetheless, in today's world, it is absolutely essential. We all know by now that abstinence from sexual activity is the surest way to avoid sexually transmitted diseases. However if you are reading this book, I'm sure this is not an option that you consider reasonable, practical, or doable.

So what can you do? You can visit the doctor and be examined and tested for the various STDs, particularly HIV. You can practice safer sex techniques using a latex condom or dental dam at each vaginal, oral, or anal sexual encounter. You and any new potential sexual partners you might meet should have an honest and open discussion about your sexual history and whether or not either of you have had any past behaviors that might have put you at risk. If you or your partner have an STD or have been exposed to an STD, this is information that should be shared in a calm and reasonable way.

When you meet a new potential partner to whom you want to make a commitment to a monogamous relationship, you and your partner should both be examined by a doctor and tested for the various STDs. Some men feel very peculiar about asking a woman to be tested, but most women are very grateful when a man introduces a discussion of safer sex procedures. Until you and your partner receive notification on the results of your tests, you can practice safer sex techniques at each vaginal, oral, or anal sexual encounter. If you or your partner have had sex with anyone else in the preceding six months, you should schedule a second test. Because HIV may not show up in the blood for three to six months after exposure, you and your partner should continue to use safer sex procedures until you have a second test at six months. This may seem very complicated, but it is the only wise way to approach sex in our complex world.

YOUR CONDOM IS YOUR FRIEND

Nobody is crazy about having sex with a condom, but we all know why they are so totally necessary. Perhaps you and your partner have both tested negative for all forms of STDs and are now in a monogamous relationship, and either she is using another reliable form of birth control, or you are trying to get pregnant. If that's the case, you can skip this section. But for anyone who ever uses a condom to prevent either pregnancy or disease, continue reading. Condoms will only do what they are supposed to do if they are purchased and used properly.

buying condoms

- To protect against STDs, buy latex or polyurethane condoms. Remember that natural or animal skin condoms are for birth control only and will not reduce the risk of STDs. Some people are allergic to latex; if this is the case for either you or your partner, choose polyurethane.

- Always check the expiration date on the package to make sure the condoms are still effective. Try to buy your condoms in stores where there is a rapid turnover and where the condoms are less likely to have deteriorated.

- Don't store condoms near heat or in the sun. The glove compartment in your car, for example, is probably not a good place since cars tend to heat up when parked in warm places.

- Choose the correct size.

- If you are using any additional lubrication either before or during intercourse, make sure that it is water-based (K-Y jelly, for example). Oil-based lubricants like Vaseline or baby oil can cause the latex in the condom to tear.

- Check to see whether the condom you are purchasing includes a spermicide as a lubricant. If so, there is something important that you need to know about spermicide. The most frequently used spermicide ingredient is nonoxynol-9, a very effective spermicide that will help prevent pregnancy. For many years, it was thought that nonoxynol-9 would also help prevent HIV. However, more recent information based on studies tells us that the exact opposite is true. Because it can irritate delicate skin tissue in the genital area, it may increase the risk of HIV or other STDs when having sex with an infected partner. Therefore, if you are using a condom as a means of preventing STDs, it is now advised that you not use a spermicide containing nonoxynol-9. The only spermicide alternative available in the United States at the current time is oxtoxynol-9.

PREVENTING CONDOM MISHAPS

In the real world we all inhabit, condoms sometimes fail. The percentage of these failures are small, but they carry with them some heavy consequences. A large number of these failures can be directly attributed to the way the condoms are handled and used. Here are some tips to help you prevent condom mishaps.

- Be careful how you take the condom out of its individual wrapping. Don't use scissors or any other sharp object, including your teeth, to open the package. When you go to unroll it, you will do so on your penis so don't fiddle with it beforehand.

- Condoms are applied to an erect penis, so make sure that you have your condoms where you will need them. You don't want to have to go searching. Before putting a condom on, remember to reserve a good half inch at the tip of the condom to act as a *reservoir* for ejaculate. This part will be left loose at the end of your penis. Place the condom on your penis and roll it on, holding the half inch tip to make sure that it provides ample space for ejaculate. Roll the condom all the way up your penis to the very base.

- After you have ejaculated, but before you have lost your erection, you want to pull out of your partner. Do this by holding the condom in place at the base of the penis and withdraw gently. Tie the end of the condom into a knot and discard it in a safe place to be thrown out with the garbage. Don't leave it lying around. After removing the condom, wash your penis with soap and water.

CONDOM TROUBLESHOOTING

Last night when I came, there was so much force that my semen came through the end of the condom. Why does this happen?

You didn't allow enough space at the end of the condom to serve as a reservoir. Make sure you that you leave plenty of room and don't worry about the dangling tip of the condom looking silly.

How can I make sure that semen doesn't leak out of the base of the condom?

You can usually solve this by grabbing the base of the condom as you ejaculate and pulling out immediately after the final spasm.

Why would a condom rip during sex?

Condoms have been known to literally disintegrate from oil-based lubrication, so make sure that you use only water based lubricants.

A condom rolled off the end of my penis during sex. Why?

It probably wasn't on right in the first place. Instead of rolling it on with one hand, use the first two fingers of both hands. Spread the condom and gently pull it all the way down to the base of your penis, making sure there is still enough condom left dangling at the tip.

I bought some condoms that ride up on my penis. Why?

It may be a size problem. It sounds like these are too small.

I started to withdraw, and it seemed like the tip of the condom was grabbed by my wife's vagina. It stretched out and snapped back at me. What happened?

What happened is that your partner's PC muscle did grip your penis and consequently the condom you were using. Always hold the base of the condom as you withdraw and pull out very slowly.

TALKING ABOUT BIRTH CONTROL

In many relationships, the woman is consistently the one who is in charge of birth control. After all, she is the one whose body would be most affected by a pregnancy. It's too easy for a guy to pretend that birth control is none of his business and let his partner do all of the planning. This is not an intelligent or thought-out approach. Men need to know what's going on. You need to know because it's appropriate for you to assume equal responsibility for the sexual relationship—and that includes birth control. It's also appropriate for you to know as much as possible because not all women are equally well informed, advised, sophisticated, or diligent about the various methods of avoiding contraception. Many younger women, for example, get pregnant because they do not really know how to use the birth control method they have chosen.

It's also important for men to realize that women like it when their partners have some understanding of the female body and how it works. It increases a woman's comfort zone if a man doesn't freak out, for example, because she has her period. She likes it if her partner understands the kind of stress certain birth control methods place on her body. Birth control is an important and serious subject. Couples should discuss the form of birth control they are using. If you know a woman well enough to have sex, you should know her well enough to talk about contraception. Failing to do this can have serious implications in your life. It's also a good idea to talk about what you would do as a couple if your birth control method were to fail.

Here are some birth control methods and their rate of effectiveness. I'm using numbers from Planned Parenthood.

barrier methods of contraception

The Male Condom

The male condom is estimated to be about 85 to 95 percent effective. If you combine the condom with withdrawal (keeping the condom on your penis and withdrawing before you ejaculate), that rate goes up to 100 percent.

The Female Condom

The female condom is not quite as effective as the male condom. It is considered to be 75 to 95 percent effective. This is a relatively new addition to the over-the-counter methods of birth control. It is typically sold with a non-spermicidal lubricant, and lubrication is essential for comfort. The female condom is made of polyurethane, which is helpful for those women who are sensitive to latex. It can be a little complicated to use so women who want to try it should practice and be very careful about following the directions.

Spermicide

Spermicide contains an ingredient that kills sperm. It comes in a foam, cream, jelly, film, or suppository. To use, the spermicide product is inserted deep into the vagina before intercourse. Film and suppositories feel dry, but melt when inserted into the vagina. Creams, jellies, and foams can be inserted into the vagina with a reusable applicator that is sold with the product. It's important to make certain that the package you are buying contains an applicator as some do not. All of these products should be inserted into the vagina within twenty minutes of having sex. These products should be reinserted each time you have sex. According to Planned Parenthood numbers, spermicide is 71 to 85 percent effective. Combining spermicides with condoms boosts the effectiveness of these methods of birth control and it is recommended that you do so.

Many women complain that spermicides cause their vaginas to itch and burn. Often this sensation is temporary and disappears within a few minutes. But for some women it lasts and causes a good deal of irritation.

Spermicides have a really icky taste. Keep that in mind if you are planning on having oral sex.

The Diaphragm

The diaphragm is a soft latex or rubber cup that is inserted into the vagina and covers the cervix. A diaphragm needs to be prescribed by a doctor after an examination to ascertain the correct type and size. The diaphragm is more effective as a contraceptive if spermicidal cream or jelly is also applied. After you have sex, it is advised that the diaphragm stay in place for up to eight hours. If you want to have sex again, more cream or jelly needs to be inserted into the vagina, using an applicator, while the diaphragm stays in place. Although a diaphragm should stay in place for at least six hours after sex, it must be removed within twenty-four hours to avoid serious bacterial infections.

The diaphragm needs to be replaced at least once every two years, or sooner if it shows any signs of deterioration. The size also needs to be checked regularly, particularly if a woman gains or loses weight.

How well a woman uses a diaphragm determines its level of effectiveness. Sixteen out of a hundred women who use the diaphragm will become pregnant during the first year of use. With perfect use, that number drops to six out of a hundred.

The Cervical Cap

The cervical cap, also prescribed by a doctor, is similar to the diaphragm in that it is inserted into the vagina and fits over the cervix. Like the diaphragm, spermicide increases its reliability. Its effectiveness is similar to the diaphragm in women who have never given birth, but it is significantly less effective for women who have given birth.

The Shield

Another prescription item, the shield is a cup-like device that fits over the cervix with a loop that aids in removal. It also is more effective when used with a spermicide.

The diaphragm, cap, and shield have a drawback for some women who may experience an increase in bladder infections. In some instances, the sexual position and angle of penetration can cause the diaphragm, cap, or shield to change position, thus reducing effectiveness. Women who are allergic to latex may not be able to use the diaphragm or the cervical cap. Also, some people complain that they are aware of the cap and shield during intercourse and it causes discomfort. The diaphragm, cap, and shield are not effective when a woman is menstruating.

Another reminder about latex: petroleum-based products and many oils and lotions will weaken latex products which could then break or tear.

---

hormone-based birth control products

Depo-Provera

This is an injection of hormones containing synthetic progesterone; it will prevent pregnancy for three months. In order for Depo-Provera to be effective, you have to be very disciplined about visiting a medical professional on schedule every three months. It is considered to be 99.7 percent effective as a birth control method.

Depo-Provera has some drawbacks in that a large percentage of women gain weight while using it. Another problem is that for women who want to get pregnant, fertility may not return immediately once they stop getting the injections. It can take up six to twelve months for fertility to return. There are several other hormone-related side effects that a women needs to discuss with her doctor. As with most hormonal forms of birth control, some women report mood changes.

Birth Control Pills

There are different kinds of pills available to women, all of which include hormones. Birth control pills are 92 to 99.7 percent effective, which makes them very appealing, but they can have side effects ranging from headaches and sore breasts to weight gain. There are also some rare, but very serious, potential health risks, including blood clots, heart attack, and stroke. Smokers over age thirty-five, run the greatest risk.

Birth control pills only work when a woman remembers to take them. If you are nervous about pregnancy, don't be nervous about reminding your partner. Become informed about the kind of birth control pill she uses and the potential risks of the hormones involved. Discuss these with her. As a woman gets older, she sometimes runs a greater risk of some of the side effects. Does your partner want to run these risks? Do you want her to do so?

There are other methods of birth control that depend on hormones. These include the ring, which is inserted into the vagina for three weeks and then taken out for a week, and the patch, a plastic patch that releases hormones. A new patch is placed on the skin every week for three weeks. Nothing is used for the fourth week. Users of the ring and the patch need to talk to their doctors about possible side effects, which may be similar to those users of the pill experience.

Hormone-based methods of birth control are not only effective, they are convenient since they allow for a certain amount of sexual spontaneity. However, as with all forms of birth control, your partner should discuss them in detail with her doctor so that she is aware of all the pros and cons. You should then ask that she discuss them with you.

intrauterine devices (IUDs)

An IUD is a small device that a doctor inserts into a woman's uterus through the cervix. Although there is typically a small string that hangs down from the IUD into the upper part of the vagina, it should not be noticeable during sex. IUDs, which can last for up to ten years, prevent pregnancy by changing the way the egg and sperm interact. They are considered to be 98 to 99 percent effective as a birth control method.

There are two well-known forms of IUDs. One is called the Copper T because it includes slim copper wire. The other type releases small amounts of synthetic progesterone. There are a group of possible side effects to the IUD, including more difficult menstrual periods. These should all be carefully discussed with a doctor.

BONUS POINTS TO YOU

In many monogamous committed relationships where there is little concern about STDs, a woman may assume most of the responsibility for birth control. She may take hormones; she may have hormone injections; she may have a little plastic thing-a-ma-bob inserted into her uterus; she may put devices into her vagina before she has sex; she may regularly fill her vagina with spermicidal creams. This is a huge responsibility that takes time and energy and discipline. Whatever form of birth control is chosen, a woman may experience a wide variety of possible side effects. In short, it's a lot of work and it can be a real pain.

Women appreciate it when a man understands what is involved in birth control. They appreciate it when a man takes the time to both discuss and understand all the ramifications of the form of birth control his partner uses. Men who are able to do this get bonus points in the great lover department.

index